The Complete
Babysitter's Handbook

Rita Leydon

The Complete Babysitter's Handbook

Elizabeth James
&
Carol Barkin

Illustrated by Rita Flodén Leydon

WANDERER BOOKS

Published by Simon & Schuster, New York

Designed by Elizabeth Woll
Manufactured in the United States of America
10   9   8   7   6   5   4   3

WANDERER and Colophon are trademarks
of Simon & Schuster

Library of Congress Cataloging in Publication Data

Barkin, Carol.
    The complete babysitter's handbook.

    Bibliography: p.
    Includes index.
    SUMMARY: Advice for the young baby sitter including
how to get jobs, how to deal with parents, safety precautions, handling the children, and dealing with
emergencies.
    1. Baby sitters—Juvenile literature.   [1. Baby
sitters] I. James, Elizabeth, joint author.
II. Leydon, Rita Flodén. III. Title.
HQ769.5.B37   649'.1'0248   80-12350

ISBN 0-671-33067-5

To our parents who encouraged us to be babysitters,
and
To our brothers and sister who suffered through
our first attempts

Contents

CONTENTS

PART III.   YOU, THE PROFESSIONAL   79

PART IV.   CLIENT WORKSHEETS   103

Introduction

Your *Complete Babysitter's Handbook* package is a survival guide to babysitting for fun and profit. The book itself covers everything you need to know about landing jobs and doing the work with confidence and enthusiasm. Read it through to get the overall picture. Then take it with you on each job and use the index to find answers to specific questions.

The Client Worksheets at the back of the book are tools especially designed for this book. They provide an easy way to organize information on each of the families you babysit for. Using the Worksheets, you won't forget that Johnny Jones is allergic to milk and Susie Smith needs a hat in summer because she sunburns easily! You'll have this information right in front of you.

The Client Worksheets cover all aspects of your job. Of course, you won't need answers to every question for each family. Glance through the Worksheets and see which questions are appropriate for the family you're sitting for. If you think of other questions, so much the better; jot them down on that family's Worksheet. (When your business starts to boom and you need more Worksheets, just make Xerox copies of a blank one.) The idea is to find out what you need to know so you won't have to ask a two-year-old how to work the stove. The more you find out about each job before the parents leave, the more relaxed you'll be when you're left in charge of the kids.

Clip a pen to your Handbook and take the whole package with you whenever you go babysitting. With your Client Worksheets filled out, you're all set for a successful career as a top-notch babysitter.

PART I

You and the Parents

The Most Popular Babysitter in Town

Of all the available babysitters, what will make you the person Mrs. Jones calls first?

Everyone's favorite babysitter is the one who really enjoys the job. And the best part of babysitting is that the more fun you have doing it, the more jobs you'll get.

It may seem surprising that by having more fun, you'll get more work. But it's true! Obviously, if you spend the afternoon listening to squabbling, screaming, and sobbing, your charges aren't enjoying themselves much, and neither are you. On the other hand, if you have a good time with the kids, chances are they're happy too. They'll want to see you again, and they'll let their parents know.

You may think it will be hard to compete for jobs with experienced grandmotherly types. But actually you have many advantages. You have much more energy than an older person, and that's a big plus when you're dealing with young children. Also, you're probably more flexible—you haven't had years to develop rigid methods of handling kids. This means you can approach each child as an individual and easily go along with a particular family's routine. Another advantage is that you're not that many years older than your charges. You can probably remember what it was like to be a little kid, and you can understand what makes them happy or sad. And don't forget, younger children tend to hero-worship teenagers—they'll often imitate the things you do, which can make your job much easier.

Some of the best babysitters are boys. Does that surprise you? It shouldn't! In addition to being able to care for children as well as girls, boys often have skills and interests that many girls don't—an encyclopedic knowledge of baseball or the physical strength to help young Karen ride her new two-wheeler. You can have a great time on a rainy Saturday afternoon explaining the fine points of the televised UCLA-USC game to an avid nine-year-old fan. And babysitting provides terrific experience for a summer job as a camp counselor, Little League coach, or lifeguard.

Keep in mind too that divorced and widowed mothers are often eager to hire a boy sitter. Children whose fathers are not living at home can benefit from an older male's companionship.

Of course, anyone who babysits has to take the responsibilities seriously. Parents must feel confident leaving their children's safety and well-being in your hands.

What else do parents look for in a babysitter? You can probably think of a number of things yourself: friendliness, interest in younger children, honesty, punctuality, patience, the ability to be kind but firm, respect for other people's privacy and possessions, sensitivity to children's needs, and a good supply of common sense.

Talk over your ideas with your own parents. They've probably had a lot of experience with babysitters. Ask them what qualities made them choose one babysitter over another. You may pick up some valuable tips on making your customers happy.

Attitude is everything in this job. When parents know that you like their children and are happy to spend time with them, and when they know that you can be trusted, you'll have more jobs than you can handle.

Rita Leydon

Look Before You Leap

You've decided that babysitting sounds like a pretty good way to make some extra money. And you're right! But now what? First, take some time to think things through so you'll know what types of jobs you want to take and what situations you'll feel comfortable with.

For example, are your afternoons free for babysitting, or are you all tied up with music lessons, swim-team practice, drama club rehearsals, or the student council? Go over your own family's ground rules with your parents. Will they object to weeknight babysitting? How about weekends? Can you take a job that will last until 2 A.M., or do you have to be home by midnight?

Try to be realistic about how much time you have available for work. You can't count on getting your homework done while you're babysitting. Your job as a sitter is to entertain and take care of the children, and they're not likely to enjoy watching you write your social studies paper! After the kids go to bed, of course, you'll have time to study, but what if this is the night little Debbie has a nightmare?

Don't forget that you have your own social life. You won't have much time for your friends if you take on babysitting jobs every afternoon and evening. Making money hand over fist won't be worth it if you're failing all your classes and your friends think you're ignoring them. So go slowly at first until you see how much you can take on.

Here's something else to think about. Do you like children of all ages? You may not know yet which age groups appeal to you most, and you won't want to limit yourself too much—you probably won't find many jobs if you decide to sit only with five-year-olds. But, on the other hand, if handling tiny babies makes you nervous, why not pass up those job opportunities until you feel more sure of yourself around infants? And if changing dirty diapers really turns you off, you'd better stick with children over three years old. You'll enjoy babysitting more if you don't overestimate what you can handle.

But don't sell yourself short. You have a lot more to offer than you realize. Even if you can't carry a tune, your enthusiasm is what counts—kids love learning new songs and they won't notice if you're off-key. When you sit down to crayon with Timmy, your friendly interest and the shared experience matter much more to him than how well you can actually draw. As you play with your charges, you may be the first to realize that Suzie is ready for tic-tac-toe. Tell her parents; they'll be thrilled —with Suzie *and* you!

Simply because you're older, you know a lot more than the kids you take care of. Children are curious about everything and they'll want to learn new things from you. So go ahead and teach them. It's pretty boring to sit in a chair and watch kids play; you'll all have a lot more fun if you get down on the floor and help them figure out how to build a block tower. Don't be embarrassed to join in and give them the benefit of your experience.

Besides being fun and profitable, babysitting has some bonuses you may not have thought of. First, the experience of looking for jobs and meeting prospective employers will come in handy when you're looking for a part-time or full-time job later on. Babysitting is terrific preparation for other kinds of work with children—summer camp counselor, nursery school assistant teacher, or summer park program employee. In addition, a parent you've babysat for often will be happy to write a letter of reference; this recommendation may be very helpful when you're applying for a regular job.

Have you thought about how much you'll be learning while you babysit? In addition to finding out about how children grow and develop, you'll be absorbing information about lifestyles that may be different from your family's. You'll probably never again have the chance to be part of the intimate day-to-day life in so many different homes. Keep your eyes open, both for the ideas you'd like to make use of in your own life and for the problems you'd like to avoid.

Once you've figured out the best way to fit babysitting into your schedule, you're ready to break into the job market.

Breaking Into the Job Market

Now that you know what you want to do, it's time to look for customers. Maybe someone has already asked you to babysit for her children. If so, that's a good start. After you've worked for that family once or twice, you can ask them to let their friends know that you're available. Word of mouth is a terrific way of getting more work. Parents are likely to call you if they've heard from their friends that you're a good babysitter, and you'll feel more comfortable about accepting a job from people you don't know if they are friends of a family you've already worked for. And perhaps your own parents will spread the word that you're available.

Be sure and tell your own friends too that you're looking for babysitting work. Then, if one of them can't accept a job, he or she might recommend you instead. This is an easy way of expanding your contacts with potential employers.

But what if you don't have any leads at all? If you're just starting out as a babysitter, it might be a good idea to volunteer your services. Go to your own church or temple or to one in your neighborhood; find out if they need someone to watch youngsters while their parents attend services. As a volunteer, you'll be working for free, but you'll be gaining valuable experience and making lots of contacts for future jobs.

Other groups you might ask about volunteering are your local library and neighborhood Brownie, Campfire Girls, and Cub Scout troops. Perhaps the children's librarian would like to have a story hour once a week. Again, this is a great way to meet prospective customers, and you'll also learn a lot about entertaining small children. Any group leader or den mother would love to have some help; as an assistant leader, you'll widen your pool of families to babysit for.

Don't forget that, as an extra benefit, community volunteer work looks great on applications for scholarships, student exchange programs, and college admission.

Be creative! Try to think of other places where a little investment of your time can result in lots of new jobs. For instance, does your community have a Welcome Wagon or other introductory program for newcomers? Local businesses donate small gifts or discount coupons so that people who are new in town will shop in their stores. Why not ask if you can donate an hour or two of free babysitting to families who have just moved in? Any mother would be delighted to have you keep her kids out from under her feet while she unpacks the good china or cleans out the attic. You needn't be experienced to do this—you'll be in her home and she'll be right there in the house to supervise. If the Welcome Wagon people are willing to include your service, make up some coupons for them to hand out.

FREE

2 Hours of Babysitting

In Your New Home

I'll Keep Your Kids Amused

While You Unpack!

Suzie Smith   901-7492

Rita Leydon

How about if you have some babysitting experience but you're looking for more customers? Perhaps you've just moved to a new city and you don't know anyone yet. Contact the local Y and find out if they need babysitters for the children of people who are taking classes there. If they don't already provide this service, maybe they'd like to start.

You may also find a job in private exercise and dance classes where you can entertain the kids while Mom stretches and bends. In fact, many such schools already offer babysitting for their clients, and they may need an assistant.

A good way to find jobs is to advertise. Churches, temples, Y's, and community service organizations may keep lists of babysitters for their members. Call to find out about this. To get your name on the list, you'll probably have to go for an interview. Sometimes these places give classes in babysitting and keep lists of those who take the course. Babysitting classes are usually free or very inexpensive, and it's nice to be able to tell a nervous parent that you've completed the course. A typical three-session course might include a class on safety with a police detective and a firefighter, a class on infant care with a pediatric nurse, and a session with a nursery school director on playing with young children and understanding them.

Ask at your church or Y if you can put up a notice on the bulletin board. Think about other places where parents of young children often go—a library bulletin board might be a good spot, or the office of a neighborhood nursery school (you'll have to ask if it's okay to post your ad), or the community bulletin board of a private swim club.

Many families need a sitter to pick up kids when school is over and take care of them until a working parent gets home. This is a regular job, five days a week; you might want to share it with a friend. Ask at the local elementary school or after-school program. They may know a family that needs a sitter, or they may let you put up a notice on a bulletin board.

Keep on the lookout for other possibilities. Maybe your family's pediatrician would be willing to recommend you as a babysitter for other patients.

You've probably noticed other people's ads in grocery stores and laundromats. Before you try this, and before putting an ad in a newspaper, talk it over with your parents. They may feel it is too risky to publish your name and phone number. It's not the same as posting your name at a church or synagogue. Anyone who answers an ad from these places won't be a total stranger; even if you don't know them, you'll know someone who does. It's sad but true that in any community there are people whose homes you would not want to go to alone. In your eagerness to find customers, don't forget this fact of life.

One of the best ways to find babysitting jobs is through an employment service for teenagers. Many communities have such programs, run by the Chamber of Commerce, the town council, or the school system. Usually this is a free service—you register for the kind of work you want, and the employment service puts you in touch directly with people who have a job to fill.

You can register for other jobs in addition to babysitting—party helper, house and lawn work, snow shoveling, and even Christmas card addressing. This kind of program is a valuable resource for any community, both for teenagers who want jobs and for adults who don't know whom to call when they need a babysitter.

If your community doesn't have such a service, encourage someone to set one up. Talk to your school principal, the head of your PTA, or someone at the Chamber of Commerce. You might even find that a service club such as Rotary, the Elks, or Kiwanis would be interested in sponsoring a youth employment program.

Being Businesslike Pays Off

When someone calls and asks you to babysit, are you prepared? This is how *not* to sound on the phone.

> YOU: Hello?
>
> MRS. AMES: Hello, is this Jane Goodwin?
>
> YOU: Yes.
>
> MRS. AMES: This is Mrs. Ames. I saw your ad on the library bulletin board. We're new in town and I need a babysitter for next Friday evening. Are you free then?
>
> YOU: Yeah, sure.
>
> MRS. AMES: Oh, good. My daughter Laura is just a year old. Have you sat with babies this age?
>
> YOU: Yeah, I think so. Let's see, the Jones kids—no, they're older. Hm, wait a minute, who were those people? Oh, the Petersons. I think Jimmy is a year old.
>
> MRS. AMES: Fine, maybe I could give them a call. Do you have their number?
>
> YOU: Uh, no, I guess I don't. Maybe you could look it up.
>
> MRS. AMES: Well, how much do you charge?

YOU: Gee, I don't know. Mostly people pay me what they think is about right.

MRS. AMES (*sounding doubtful*): Okay. We're going to go out at seven o'clock, so I'd like you to come at quarter of. Can you get here yourself? We live at 731 Maple Street.

YOU: I guess so. I'll probably be able to find someone to give me a ride.

MRS. AMES: All right. So we'll see you here at six forty-five next Friday.

YOU: Oh, my gosh, I just remembered, I'm going to my grandmother's for dinner that night. Sorry.

Mrs. Ames is not likely to call you again. She won't recommend you to anyone she talks to, either. Naturally, the most important part of babysitting is how well you take care of the children. But if the first impression you give is that you're disorganized and irresponsible, not many parents will feel they can leave you alone with their children. So get it together and sound like you know what you're doing.

Find out from other babysitters what the going rate is in your area, so you'll be able to say definitely how much you charge per hour. There is usually an hourly rate that most sitters in a community charge; if you ask for more than this, you'll lose a lot of work, but if you charge less, you're just cheating yourself. So ask around.

You may find that there are different rates for different working conditions. Maybe nighttime rates are lower than daytime, since the children are asleep and you can read or do homework, but sometimes the rates are raised after midnight. Or the rate may be higher if there are more than two or three children to take care of. See what experienced sitters in your community say about this. Then, once you've settled on a rate or rates, stick to your decision.

A Word About Housework

When you babysit, a certain amount of general cleanup is part of the job. If you fix a meal for the kids and/or yourself, you should wash whatever dishes you've used. After the children are in bed, you'll put away the toys, games, and books that are scattered around the house. In other words, most parents expect you to clean up any mess you and the kids have created.

On the other hand, doing the laundry, vacuuming, washing the kitchen floor, and shoveling snow are definitely not part of your job. Parents you sit for regularly may occasionally rush out to catch an early movie and leave the sink full of dirty dinner dishes. You certainly don't have to wash them, but if you want to do it after the kids are asleep, it's a nice extra to give your customers. But if this kind of thing is routinely expected of you, you're being taken advantage of. Either don't do it or charge extra for the time you spend on housework.

Your job, after all, is to take care of the children. You can't do that and do housework at the same time. If you find that this is becoming a frequent problem, it's easiest to handle it on the phone before you take the job. You might ask, "Will you want me to do anything besides taking care of the children?" If the answer is yes, say, "I charge more for housework," and adjust your rates accordingly. Another approach is to say, "I don't feel I can do a responsible job of babysitting while I'm cleaning the house, so I'll only be able to do it if there's time after the children are asleep." Although you may never run into this problem, you should decide in advance what you will do if it comes up.

Get Organized!

Get into the habit of keeping track of all your commitments—school, social, and babysitting—on a large calendar. You can get free ones from banks and many other businesses. Mrs.

Jones will have a lot more confidence that you've got your head screwed on straight if you say, "Just a minute—let me check my calendar." If it's all written down, you won't run the risk of accepting a babysitting date only to remember later in the week that that's the day you're supposed to play cornet in the school band concert. You also won't commit the worst offense in any parent's eyes—forgetting a babysitting appointment entirely.

Here's how to handle that important first phone call from a new customer. Don't be shy. As soon as you find out she's asking you to babysit, ask her to hang on for a moment. Then proceed as follows:

Pull out a pencil and your calendar, and turn to a new Client Worksheet at the back of your Handbook. Now you're ready to take down all the information you need, and you won't have to ask Mrs. Brown to repeat herself.

First, make sure you're free to take the job. If you are, write down the "temporary" information on your calendar:

- What time to arrive

- When your client expects to come home

This information will apply only to the appointment you're making; it will vary each time you babysit.

Be sure to note your client's name on the calendar too; it's easy to forget whether you're going to Mrs. Brown's on Monday and Mrs. Smith's on Saturday or the other way around!

Next, get the "permanent" information and write it in on your Client Worksheet. You will take this Worksheet with you when you go to babysit. You need to know:

- Customer's name, address, and phone number (you'll be upset if you forget how to spell Mrs. Sczymancski's name and don't have her phone number to call and say you're in the hospital with a broken leg for a week!)

- Children's names and ages

Rita Leydon

If your client is not going to call for you, you'll need to find out how to get to the house if you're unfamiliar with the address. And make sure you know what arrangements will be made to get you home. It's customary for the parents to walk or drive you home or to pay for your taxi—even if you live just around the corner. The people you sit for want to know that you get home safely. (Note how you will get home on the Appointment Schedule at the bottom of the first page of the Worksheet since this may vary each time you babysit. After you hang up, copy the temporary information that you wrote on your calendar onto the Appointment Schedule. It's a good idea to have a duplicate record, and eventually you'll get an idea of how often the client is calling you and how much money you're earning.)

By this time you'll probably know whether you plan to charge more than your standard rate. If all three kids are having overnight guests and the dog has a new litter of puppies, you'll want to charge a bit extra! In any event, make sure you and your client agree on the rate of pay before you hang up.

If your client lives in your immediate neighborhood, you can probably fill in the emergency phone numbers (fire, police, ambulance, and poison control center) from your own phone book. In any case, BE SURE this information is completely filled in before the parents leave the house where you are sitting.

Don't forget to write down the name and phone number of your family doctor; if for some reason you can't reach a child's own doctor, it's good to have someone else to call. And write down your own home phone number on this sheet; it may seem silly, but in an emergency your mind may go blank. It's best to have everything written down where you can find it quickly.

What About Cancellations?

Presumably you won't have to cancel your babysitting commitments very often. The whole point of keeping a calendar is to avoid conflicts with other jobs or social events. But occasionally a cancellation can't be helped—you might have to go to a funeral, for example, or you might get the flu. Never babysit when you're sick. It's not fair to pass on those bugs to the children, and besides, you won't be in shape to do a good job.

If you must cancel, let your employers know as early as you possibly can. Scout around to see if you can find someone to take your place. Then you'll be in a position to say, "I'm sorry I can't come myself. If you don't have someone else you want to call, my friend Tim Hunter is free that night and he's an experienced babysitter." This way you will have done what you can to fulfill your commitment and these parents will be willing to call you again.

Rita Leydon

Ready for Action

Babysitting can sometimes be a little messy. You won't want to play on the floor in your dry-clean-only white pants, and you certainly won't want to feed a drooling baby in your best silk shirt. Wear sensible, washable clothes so you can relax and have fun with the kids. Blue jeans are fine. Parents don't expect you to get all dressed up. (On the other hand, they will expect your clothes to be clean, and they'll be somewhat put off if you show up in your low-cut see-through top and your skimpiest short shorts!)

If you are sitting with babies, don't wear necklaces, pointed pins, or dangly earrings. Little babies can clutch these shimmering items faster and more tenaciously than you might think is possible.

If you are not being picked up by your client, leave yourself enough time to arrive promptly, or even a few minutes early. This will give you a chance to say hi to the kids before their parents leave and to get any last-minute instructions. The parents will want to leave at the time they've planned on, so your promptness will be appreciated. In fact, with a new customer, it's a good idea to arrive ten to fifteen minutes early; this gives you time to find out all you'll need to know.

Be sure you've left a note for your parents with the name, address, and phone number of the people you're sitting for and what time you expect to be home. This is just common sense as well as common courtesy.

Think about what you want to take with you on the job. If the children are going to be asleep, you'll probably have time to do some homework, read a book, or work on that sweater you're knitting for Dad.

Take this Handbook and a pencil with you. It's also a good idea to invest in a small flashlight and carry it in your pocket or purse. If there's a power failure or even a burnt-out light, you won't want to fumble around searching for a flashlight in a strange house. Remember, too, that since you won't be in your own home, you should take an extra sweater with you if you think it might be drafty. Keep a few Band-Aids in your wallet or purse; they often come in handy.

It's good to have a little money with you, preferably in coins. That way you'll have change if it's necessary when the parents pay you. This is something a lot of sitters don't think of doing, but parents notice this kind of consideration. Another reason to have some money with you is in case of an emergency. What if the bus breaks down on the way to your job and you need to call and let your client know you'll be late?

Finally, you might consider putting together a surprise bag as part of your babysitting equipment. Nothing breaks the ice faster with young children than something new to play with, and your collection will help distract them as their parents leave.

You can do this for practically no money. Use your imagination and rescue potential playthings before they're thrown into the trash. Keep on the lookout for:

- Disposable aluminum baking dishes—great for cymbals

- Cardboard paper towel tubes—terrific horns or spyglasses or drumsticks for aluminum pans

- Plastic lids (with or without bottoms)—stack them, roll them, use for "stepping stones"

- Small cardboard jewelry or stationery boxes, cigar boxes, small metal tins (like tea tins)—fun to open and close and hide things in or great for collections of all sorts

- Cigar bands—make fabulous rings

- Plastic bottles—wash them well and put in a few dried beans or some rice for a rattle (make sure top is on *tight*)

- Books—from the library or your attic; a new story is always a treat

With the addition of inexpensive balloons and some pipe cleaners to make animal figures for older children, you'll be the most welcome babysitter in town.

Checklist

Do you have everything you need when you walk out the door?

- This book
- Client Worksheet
- Pencil
- Small flashlight
- Extra sweater
- Band-Aids
- Money (coins)
- Surprise bag
- Homework, book, knitting

RITA LEYDON

First Get the Facts

When you arrive, there is certain information you must be sure to get from the parents before they leave: the phone number where they can be reached, the phone numbers of their doctor and a neighbor or relative you can call in an emergency. Many families have these numbers written on a pad or bulletin board beside the phone. Whether they do or don't, be sure to write them on your Client Worksheet. You'll probably never have to use them, but if you do, you won't have time to waste paging through the phone book.

Ask the parents if they are expecting any phone calls or visitors; if so, write down any messages they want you to pass along.

Getting Your Bearings

If this is the first time you've babysat in this house, you'll want to know where things are. Find out where the telephone and light switches are, and how to work the heating system and any kitchen appliances you'll be using. Make sure you know where the children's rooms and the bathroom are, and where their toys, clothes, and diapers are kept. Also find out where the first-aid supplies are. Clarify what you're expected to do and when

—what time should you feed them? do they need baths? when are their bedtimes? can they watch TV? if so, what programs?

Ask if the children need any medication or special foods. Go over their special routines with favorite stories and toys, and check on restrictions—can they have juice before bedtime? are they allowed to throw balls in the house? are there snack limitations? is there a bedtime ritual?

If the family has pets, find out if they will need any attention from you. Do you have to feed the dog or cats or let them out? Make sure you know the rules. Are the hamsters really allowed to run around loose in Tommy's bedroom? Does the Great Dane sleep in Jenny's bed? Do ask your employers to introduce you formally to any large dog— you don't want him to think he has to protect the kids from you!

Naturally you can't find out all about the family's day-to-day life in five minutes. But the more you know, the easier your job will be. Write it all down as soon as you can on your Client Worksheet, so you won't forget it.

Use your Worksheet as a guide to remind you of questions you want to ask. Of course you won't need to ask all of them on every job; if it's midwinter, questions about outdoor pools and sunscreen lotions probably won't be necessary! Don't feel you must ask every single question on the Worksheet; use your own judgment to figure out what's important. On the other hand, don't feel that these are the only questions you can ask. If something occurs to you that's not included on the Worksheet, ask! And *write down* the answer. The idea is to find out as much as you can that will help you take good care of the children and fit in smoothly with the family routines.

Some Precautionary Measures

Obviously, if the phone rings while you're babysitting, you will answer it. Here are some hints on phone safety.

Find out who's calling. It's not practical to pretend the people you're sitting for are at home but unavailable to talk on the phone. However, before you tell someone what time they'll be home or where they've gone, ask who it is—get a name and phone number. Get as much of a message as you can, and try to find out if your employers should return the call that night. Some people don't seem to like to leave phone messages, but do your best.

Don't give out unnecessary information. If the call is obviously a wrong number, never tell the caller the name of your employers, your own name, or the actual phone number they have reached. If the caller asks, "What number is this?" your answer should always be, "What number did you want?" Similarly, if the caller asks who you are, say, "Whom did you want to talk to?"

This is not being rude. The person on the other end is the one who placed the call, and he knows whom he was trying to reach. You have no obligation to tell him who or where you are.

In addition, if someone calls and says he or she is conducting a survey, immediately say you're not interested and hang up. Don't let yourself get drawn into answering questions of any kind.

Hang up on obscene or annoying calls. People who make these calls delight in hearing your anger and fear, so deprive them of this sick pleasure. As soon as you're sure it's a crank call, just hang up. There's nothing you can do about tracing these calls. You might want to jot down the time it happened, and be sure to tell your employers about it when they return.

Try not to let such a call upset you. It is unnerving, but if you hang up calmly, the caller is not very likely to call back, and he's certainly not going to show up at the door.

While we're on the subject of safety, here are some pointers on handling people who knock at the door while you're babysitting.

Don't let anyone come inside. Unless it's someone your employers told you to expect or someone you know personally, never let anyone come into the house. You may sometimes feel you're being overly rude and suspicious. But even if a woman says she lives around the corner and her house is on fire, say, "Tell me your address and I'll be glad to call the fire department for you." If it's a man (even in a uniform) to read the electric meter, tell him he'll have to come back another time. Your job is to protect the children you're sitting for, and you can't take chances with that responsibility. Better to be overcautious, even if you're sure the person is telling the truth.

Don't open the door to everyone. Even though you won't let anyone *into* the house, you may feel like an idiot if you're sitting in plain sight by the picture window and the uniformed mail carrier is outside with his official truck at the curb. *Use your judgment about opening the door.* Keep the chain on if you have any doubts at all, and again, don't let anyone inside. But you can sign for a special delivery letter or a package; the people you are sitting for will probably be glad you did.

Everyone who rings the doorbell is not a mad strangler. But people who do come usually want to talk to the owners of the house. Don't feel bad about ignoring the Fuller Brush man or religious missionaries with free literature—they'll come back some other time.

What Are Your Privileges?

Most of your employers will tell you to help yourself to snacks and soft drinks from the refrigerator. Go ahead and eat, but don't overdo it—leave them something for breakfast! Do use some judgment. No one will mind if you finish up the potato chips, but they won't be pleased if you eat up all the expensive chocolates from Switzerland.

If the parents don't mention television, ask if you may watch it after the children go to bed. This will remind them to tell you about any quirks or special features it may have. Watch whatever you want, but keep the volume down and don't get so engrossed that you won't hear Jimmy fall out of bed.

By the way, if you're the type who gets petrified watching scary movies, don't let yourself start watching one!

As for the phone, any local calls you really need to make are fine, but keep them short and don't overdo it. You can't pay attention to your job if you're involved in a heavy gossip session. And it doesn't make a very good impression on your employers if they are calling you and can't reach their own home. Don't make any toll or long-distance calls; save those for your own phone bill.

What to do about your friends coming over while you're babysitting? This can be tricky, and families have different attitudes about it. Some employers may feel you should stick to the job and not be distracted by anyone else. Others may not mind if you have a friend over to work on a school project or just to keep you company on Saturday night. Almost every parent draws the line at one friend—more than that makes it a party and that's not what they're paying you for. Don't even consider inviting your boyfriend or girlfriend over for a romantic evening after the kids are asleep. Your employers want to feel that you're treating this as a time to work, not to socialize.

Since you're working in someone else's home, it's up to you to go along with their ways of doing things. The more you find out in advance, the less you'll have to worry about. You'll be free to enjoy yourself and your job, and they'll feel confident about leaving you in charge of their home and their children.

Checklist

Here's what you need to find out about before the parents leave:

- Emergency information
- Messages and visitors expected
- Lights, telephone, heat, and appliances
- Layout of house—where things are kept
- Children's routines and restrictions
- Pets
- Your privileges

PART II

You and the Kids

Rita Leydon

First Impressions

When you meet young children for the first time, it's a good idea to take things slowly. Give them time to size you up; try to let them approach you. Kids are often a little wary of strangers, especially people bigger and older than themselves. They know that your arrival means Mom is going out, so they may not be at all happy to see you.

Don't let it bother you, and don't try so hard to make friends that you smother them with phony affection. One way to break the ice is to get down on the floor and start playing with one of the child's toys. He may come over and take it away from you, but at least you've started to make contact. Or you could say, "Gee, this is neat. Can you show me how it works?" Many children can't resist an invitation to show off their skill or knowledge.

Another ploy is to ask a child, "Will you show me your room?" If you hold out your hand as you say this, she's quite likely to take it and lead you through the house. Children take pride in showing you *their* room, *their* bed, and so on; since the parents will want you to see where everything is anyway, take advantage of the opportunity.

This technique of asking the child to show you where something is or how it works is useful in any situation. It gives the child a chance to show off his knowledge and be helpful.

You're much more likely to get his cooperation if you ask for his help instead of telling him what to do. It also lessens the possibility of your ending up in a contest of wills with the child —a contest you will probably lose.

While the parent and child are showing you around, keep your eyes open for things they forget to mention. If the child's window is open, are you supposed to close it when he goes to bed? Also observe how the parent deals with the child. If he climbs right up on his changing table and Mom doesn't bat an eye, then you'll know it's okay when he does it later. No parent can possibly remember to tell you everything about her child's behavior and stage of development. So pick up as many clues as you can before he or she leaves. Even in those few minutes, you'll get an idea of how this family does things. Then you'll be able to fit into their routine and not confuse the child by lots of changed rules and regulations.

This is important even with a very young child who supposedly will be asleep the whole time you're there. She may wake up, and she'll be upset when she sees someone she didn't expect. Besides, it'll be easier for you if you know where the diapers and dry sheets are kept instead of fumbling around in a dark room. If it's at all possible, try to meet the baby before she goes to sleep. Even if you have to show up a half hour early (for which you do not charge), it will be a good investment on your part.

It's only natural for children to be upset when their parents leave. Don't be surprised if little Suzie bursts into tears as Mom and Dad head for the door. This is particularly true of only children, who may feel as though their entire family is abandoning them. It is no reflection on your ability as a babysitter, nor does it mean the child doesn't like you.

Often the crying stops moments after the door closes. Try picking up one of the child's books and saying, "Let's sit on the couch and read a story." If she seems willing to be picked up herself, do a little cuddling—it will make both of you feel better. If you've brought along your "surprise bag" (see page 26), now is the time to open it up. There's nothing like balloon blowing or pie plate banging to take a child's mind off her troubles. But if she seems inconsolable and won't let you touch her or distract her, don't make an issue of it. Just sit on the floor calmly and cheerfully and start playing with her toys and puzzles. Eventually, she'll stop crying and join you.

It may help calm a child if you tell her that Mommy and Daddy will be back and she'll see them when she wakes up in the morning. But don't tell lies in order to reassure her. Mommy and Daddy *won't* be back right away. Even a young child remembers what you say, and when it doesn't happen, it will be hard for her to trust you about anything else.

While you are getting to know the child, he is getting acquainted with you. He may be going through a stage of asking rather peculiar personal questions. Don't let this throw you; just answer the best you can and move on to something else. Toddlers are quite interested in the differences between boys and girls and may ask some very straightforward questions. Don't be embarrassed, just answer as simply and matter-of-factly as possible. Similar questions from older children are usually a way of testing you. They know by now that people are sometimes uncomfortable talking about sex and they just want to see if they can get you flustered. If your response is a calm "I don't think that's something we need to discuss," that will be the end of it.

Older kids, too, may seem unfriendly or resentful at first; it helps to keep in mind that everyone likes to talk about his own interests and kids are no exception. Your enthusiasm about a child's hamsters, stamp collection, or coloring pad will go a long way toward establishing a rapport that will make your babysitting job fun for both of you.

Rita Leydon

Fun Within Four Walls

Most babysitting takes place indoors, and, in between meals and bedtime, you'll get to do a lot of playing with children's toys. You may be surprised at how much fun you have with blocks or dolls, and the children will appreciate your entering into their games.

One game leads to another, and you may encounter some new situations. But use your common sense to make decisions. Children do know the rules of the house, but they might be a bit imaginative in relaying them to you. If a child tells you that a game you feel is dangerous or particularly obnoxious is perfectly okay and Mom lets him do it all the time, say, "Then maybe we'll do it next time. I'll ask your mom." Then suggest an alternative activity. The parents may not, in fact, object to whatever it is the kids want to do. But check first and don't be afraid to say no.

Older children, and even some toddlers, often know exactly what they want to play or read. You won't be called upon to come up with entertainment for these children, although you may have to sharpen your own playing skills. But some kids don't have any ideas of their own or are bored with the things they've been doing and are ready to try something new. Here are some ideas for the different age groups you'll be dealing with.

Playing with Babies

Everything is a toy to a baby, even the simplest things. A ring of jingling keys can keep a baby fascinated for some time. Anything you can dangle over the crib or playpen will be a treat— just make sure it's not sharp-edged or easily breakable in case the infant gets his hands on it. Since babies tend to put anything they can into their mouths, the rule of thumb is that anything you give a baby to play with should be at least as big as his fist. Don't let him have anything that he could swallow or choke on.

Babies love bright colors; try fluttering some brightly patterned cloth as a simple mobile or tie some securely to the rails of the playpen. They also enjoy music and noises as long as they're not startlingly loud or frightening. If you're a secret shower singer, you can be a hit with baby.

For small babies the secret to success is your active entertainment. They can't do much themselves, so anything you do for them to watch and try to participate in—clapping hands, playing a toy horn, singing, making faces—will be appreciated. Older babies who are crawling or starting to crawl will love games of "rolling over," bouncing on your knee (held upright between your hands), peek-a-boo, and rolling a ball back and forth. Give these kids a few pots or pans and a wooden spoon to bang with and you'll make their day. Do you have a debate or part in the school play to rehearse? You'll never have a more appreciative audience than a baby. He won't even care what you say; he's watching your face as it moves and he enjoys the vocal contact even though he can't understand the words.

Babies are often happy just to sit on your lap and explore your face and hair with their fingers. However, they have a very short attention span. When little Craig starts fussing with boredom, pick him up and give him a look at himself in the mirror, or hand him a set of measuring cups or spoons to play with.

Babies are tougher than you think. And warmer, too. If you're comfortable with just a shirt on, little Timmy will be fine without extra layers. He doesn't need to be bundled up. You don't want to put a baby down in a draft, but he won't catch pneumonia if he's barefoot. His clothes should be loose enough for him to move around in easily.

If he bumps himself, be sympathetic but don't make a big thing of it. He's got a fair amount of natural padding and is built to handle a number of knocks. He may cry because he's startled or has scared himself, but your happy expression will reassure him that everything's fine and he'll soon be grinning.

Sometimes a baby starts to cry and can't be jollied out of it. If he doesn't have a wet diaper and he's not hungry, check to see if he's got a diaper pin jabbing him or if his clothes are binding anywhere. At times there is nothing wrong; the baby is just fretful. Rhythmic motion seems to be the best solution for this. Rock him in your lap or carry him on your shoulder about the room. You can try some gentle jiggling as you walk him. Soft singing may help. Do find out if the baby is teething. Massaging his gums with one of your (clean) fingers or giving him a teething biscuit or corner of a washcloth to chew on may make all the difference. Another possible reason for fretful crying is that the child is tired. Try putting him to bed, or rock him and sing with the lights turned down; maybe he'll just doze off.

Playing with Toddlers

These children (roughly a year and a half to three years) are a joy to be with. They are learning new things all the time and although they can walk and run, you can easily catch them. They can understand most of what you're saying; many are talking well themselves.

Toddlers will stay amused with one activity for a fairly long period of time. But they still can't entertain themselves, and although they may be quick to point out what book they want to read or drag over the toy they want to play with, you'll need to take part in all this activity. Nursery games are big with this age group—ring-around-the-rosy, peek-a-boo, patty-cake, London Bridge. Crayons and pencils hold a special fascination and you may find that "drawing" takes up lots of time. Children this age don't usually care about realistic pictures and are happy scribbling in different colors. Similarly, don't feel that you need to read the actual words in any of their books. It's enough for the two of you to be seated cozily together while the child turns the pages and you point out the pictures of various animals and cars, babies, mommies, daddies, and so on in their books. Other ideas to keep these youngsters happy are imaginary telephone conversations (don't use the real phone for this as it ties up the line and may be something Mom and Dad won't appreciate), conversations between puppets or dolls, piling lots of little toys in a truck and pushing it around the room, or simple forms of hide-and-seek. Children like to help you; you can make a game of picking up the toys and putting them away.

A toddler's life is full of bumps and falls. If you don't make a big thing of these mishaps, he'll probably go right on with what he was doing before. Make sure he's not actually bleeding. Remember, most kids this age bang into things or fall down a million times without any real injury. If he cries and it's not serious, a cuddle or a "kiss to make it better" will probably suffice.

You've no doubt heard of temper tantrums, and if you sit with toddlers, you may witness one or two. Some youngsters take this dramatic way of expressing frustration or overtiredness. Don't be alarmed. Kids don't hurt themselves while they're throwing a tantrum. Either put the child in his room or leave him where he is screaming and kicking on the floor, go to another part of the room, and ignore it. There is nothing you can do for a child while he's in the middle of this explosion. When it seems to be tapering off, go to him with a friendly offer of something else to do. Trying to discuss this behavior with the child or even referring to it won't do any good and may actually reinforce it. Just pretend it didn't happen and try to interest him in a project he can handle.

Playing with toddlers is mostly a matter of joining in. Take your cues from the child so that you won't involve him in something that's beyond his ability. It's fun to help a toddler learn new skills through play. Think of how proud he'll be when he shows Mom how he can put his puzzle pieces in all by himself.

Playing with Older Children

From about ages four or five on up, kids generally do quite a lot of playing on their own. They may have a project already under way—a model or Lego construction, a large jigsaw puzzle, a stamp or coin collection, or whatever. You may be expected only to admire their progress and to lend a hand for the hard parts.

If there are two or more children, they may work happily together without needing much assistance. An only child, however, may want you to join in and take the place of a playmate.

But what if the kids are just hanging around saying, "What can we do now?" Think back to when you were their age and see if you can come up with something that will include the whole group.

How about card games? Even younger children enjoy go fish, old maid, war, and sometimes double solitaire. Older children love hearts, canasta, and gin rummy. If you can't remember how to play these games, check your local library and brush up on the rules. Then, if the kids really enjoy card games, you can bring your cribbage board next time and teach them how to play.

Most families have a collection of board games, from checkers, chess, and backgammon to Clue or Monopoly. If the children enjoy playing, you can spend a whole evening around the board. (Don't start a game too late—nothing is more disappointing than having to go to bed when you're just about ready to buy Park Place.)

You'll want to include everyone in the activity, so save the harder games until after the younger ones have gone to bed. It's not much fun for a five-year-old to watch you and his older sister play Scrabble.

Do you know any pencil and paper games? Hangman is a perennial favorite, as are tic-tac-toe and dots-and-squares. Some of these may be new to your charges, and they'll be thrilled to learn them, especially when they beat you.

There are always guessing games to play. Everyone can have fun with warmer-colder, and you might try twenty questions and Botticelli. Or maybe the children know a game they'd like to teach you.

If you've brought along your crocheting and nine-year-old Lisa is fascinated with what you're making, why not teach her to crochet? Boys too have fun learning a new craft. This may turn out to be a huge success. Then you can suggest that next time you come, you'll help them get started on a project—place mats for Grandma or a muffler for Dad.

When everybody's tired of sitting still, try some playacting. Older kids love to create and perform skits, with you as the appreciative audience. When there are children of varying ages, you can get everybody involved in acting out "The Three Little Pigs" or "Goldilocks and The Three Bears." Get the older kids to help you coach the younger ones, and you'll all have a lot of fun.

Active indoor games of this kind are fine to work off excess energy. It's best to limit rougher indoor play, especially right before bedtime; sometimes kids get so wound up that they can't settle down and go to sleep. Also, roughhousing can quickly get out of hand. Objects can get broken and heads banged too hard before you know it. Better to be a little overcautious than to have to tell parents their stereo fell on the floor. Don't get drawn into complicated games of hide-and-seek or sardines—this can be pretty scary in a house you don't know well.

Even when the children are playing quietly on their own, you can't go off and watch TV in another room. You needn't keep your eyes glued to them every second, but be aware of what's going on. Children forget that they must not walk or run with things in their mouths or sharp objects in their hands. Remind them to go slowly and to carry scissors and sharp pencils point down. If you're alert, you'll be able to prevent unwanted contact between a running child and a fragile vase or sharp-cornered table.

Books to Read to Kids

Most kids love to be read to. And reading to them is a good way for you to develop a warm, friendly relationship with the children you're babysitting for. A perfect time to read to kids is late afternoon, when they're tired from running around in active play. And of course a story at bedtime or earlier in the evening helps them wind down and get ready for sleep.

Every child has his or her own books that you can read, but it's a special treat when you bring a new story, one they haven't heard before. When you look for a book to take along, keep the child's age in mind. A book that's too complicated will have a young child squirming in his seat and talking about something else halfway through. For any age, be sure the book you choose is short enough to be read at one sitting. You don't want to keep the kids up till eleven while you try to finish *The Wizard of Oz!* And it's not really fair to stop in the middle if you won't be around the next night to read the end.

Think back to the books you loved best when you were little. Maybe you still have them packed away somewhere and you can dig out one or two to take with you. Or go to the children's section of the library. Tell the librarian what you're looking for; she'll be happy to help you find books suitable for any age. Here are some suggestions to start you off.

BOOKS FOR TODDLERS AND PRESCHOOLERS

Collections.

• Mother Goose: There are many different editions of Mother Goose rhymes. Choose one with illustrations that appeal to you.

• Nursery tales: These are stories like "Goldilocks and the Three Bears" and "The Three Little Pigs." Check to make sure you like the way they're written—some of them sound stilted and hard to read aloud.

• Richard Scarry: Scarry is the author of many large-size books, such as *The Best Word Book Ever.* Almost every child loves poring over the busy illustrations while listening to the funny stories.

Single-story picture books. You may be overwhelmed by the vast choice of picture books in the library. Take a look at some by well-known authors: Margaret Wise Brown, Robert McCloskey, Maurice Sendak, Charlotte Zolotow. The main thing here is to make sure the text is brief enough for little ones.

Bedtime stories. Some perennial favorites are especially designed to be read just before bed. Perhaps the best loved is *Goodnight, Moon* by Margaret Wise Brown. Another good one is *Sleepy Book* by Charlotte Zolotow. Ask your librarian to recommend others.

BOOKS FOR KINDERGARTEN THROUGH SECOND GRADE

Simple fairy tales. There are easy versions of popular fairy tales like "Cinderella" and "Snow White" that are meant for this age group. But many collections of fairy tales are written in rather difficult language, so read through the stories quickly to make sure the little kids will be able to understand them.

Single-story books. This age group has a lot of fun with nonsense stories like those by Dr. Seuss: *Horton Hatches the Egg, The Cat in the Hat,* and other favorites. You'll have fun reading these yourself!

Books by Beatrix Potter are also a good bet. Everyone may already know *Peter Rabbit,* but there are plenty of others to choose from.

You can also read *Winnie the Pooh,* since each chapter is really a self-contained story.

Again, ask the librarian which books are popular with five- to seven-year-olds.

BOOKS FOR OLDER CHILDREN

Fables and fairy tales. Every library has two or three editions of Grimm's Fairy Tales, Hans Christian Andersen, and Aesop's Fables. Look through them and see which one you like. Also consider Kipling's *Just So Stories;* a child who hasn't heard these before is in for a treat. And for real fairy tale addicts, you can go through the collections by Andrew Lang: *The Red Fairy Book, The Green Fairy Book,* etc.

Stories. A number of stories that are fun for both boys and girls are short enough to read at one sitting. You can find collections of stories on a particular subject: dog stories, horse stories, adventure stories, and so on. Or you can find books of stories about a single character; try *Homer Price* or *The Merry Adventures of Robin Hood* for starters.

Books. If you babysit for the same children several times a week, you can read one chapter a day from a longer book. The choice here is endless; when selecting, think about the kinds of things the particular child is interested in. You can all have a wonderful time with the classics: *Treasure Island, Alice in Wonderland, The Wind in the Willows,* and the Oz books will hold children spellbound. Introduce children to more modern classics, such as the books by Beverly Cleary and E. B. White. Or try a mystery: Nancy Drew and the Hardy Boys are always popular.

Books on Games and Activities

If you find yourself running out of play ideas, here are the names of some books you can find in the library that are full of game suggestions for kids of all ages.

Marzollo, Jean, and Janice Lloyd. *Learning Through Play.* New York: Harper & Row (paperback), 1974.

> Even though this book is meant to be an educational tool, it contains lots of suggestions for easy games and simple toys you can make. For kids of all ages.

Members of the Staff of the Boston Children's Medical Center and Elizabeth M. Gregg. *What to Do When "There's Nothing to Do."* New York: Delacorte Press, 1970.

> This lighthearted collection is chock-full of easy-to-do games and great ideas for toys and playthings. It's arranged by age group, and it contains suggestions for reading aloud and singing as well. You'll find some new and inventive additions for your surprise bag here.

Montgomerie, Norah, compiler. *This Little Pig Went to Market.* New York: Franklin Watts, Inc., 1967.

> Here's a super collection of play rhymes for the little ones. Browse through it to refresh your memory on how to play patty-cake or "Here's the church and here's the steeple"!

Search through the 790 section of your library shelves; you'll find game and craft books for every age group. Here's where you get the rules for outdoor games, indoor games, pencil and paper games, and card games; you'll also get some ideas for craft activities that don't require much equipment.

Keeping the Peace

Like anyone else, children disagree and sometimes get into squabbles. Either let them work it out themselves or suggest a fair compromise, but don't get involved in discussion or arbitration. It won't help, and if you take one child's side, the other is bound to feel resentful.

If the argument degenerates into actual fighting, you'll have to step in. Turn a deaf ear to cries of "He hit me first!" Just separate them firmly and announce that they must play separately until they can get along. Help each of them get started on another activity. The firmer you are about this and the less you listen to explanations, the faster it will blow over and you'll all be able to do something together.

RITA LEYDON

Wide Open Spaces

When you're babysitting in the daytime, it's fun to take the kids outside whenever you can. It makes a nice change for all of you from indoor playing, and it gives kids a chance to work off some surplus energy.

Taking Babies Outside

Babies love to go outdoors—there's so much more to see. They can go out at any time of year as long as it's not pouring rain. Just make sure they are dressed appropriately for the weather.

In good weather, spend an hour or so in the backyard. Take a towel or blanket to put on the grass or use an infant seat. He'll be delighted to look around at the grass and butterflies and the leaves moving in the breeze. Take a few toys outside with you, or let the baby play with natural "toys"—a large leaf, a stone too big to swallow, a stick (don't let him put it in his mouth). He'll be fascinated watching you make a clover chain. If a big black ant crawls over his hand, don't worry about it— he'll think it's the funniest thing that ever happened.

After an hour (even less if it's hot), the baby will probably be ready for a change of scene. In summer you'll need to keep him in the shade and watch carefully for sunburn.

Babies also love to go for walks. They may even fall asleep in the carriage or stroller, but the fresh air is good for them and the exercise won't hurt you. You can just walk around the block, and the baby will be happy recognizing any familiar sights. But a nearby park or playground may be more fun— even kids who can't join in yet enjoy watching older children swing and slide and dogs chase Frisbees.

Take along whatever you might need. It's no fun to walk all the way home with a screaming baby because you forgot to bring the juice bottle. An extra diaper and a couple of the baby's washable toys can keep a pleasant outing from turning into a fiasco. If the baby is teething, take along whatever she's allowed to snack on. Be sure to walk only until you're half-tired; you've got to push that stroller all the way home!

Keep the safety straps of the stroller fastened securely at all times. A stroller isn't a very stable vehicle and can easily tip far enough for the baby to fall out. Older babies tend to be escape artists and will try to climb out when you least expect it. Take special care crossing streets. Carriages as well as strollers are hard to maneuver up and down curbs, and either contraption slows you down considerably. Of course, the baby will no doubt choose the middle of the street to drop the toy you've just handed her (this is why many parents tie toys securely to the sides of a carriage or stroller).

A stroller doesn't offer a baby much protection and it keeps her much closer to the ground than you are. Watch out for stray dogs or bushes that could scratch the baby's face, and steer clear of tempting flowers and berries that her little hands can reach. Never leave the baby alone outside for even a second.

You may walk on the same street every day on your way to school but when you push the baby along it, you'll notice things you never looked at before—a striped cat dashing across the sidewalk makes the baby point with glee, and a pair of angry squirrels produces a delighted laugh. A baby makes a great excuse for a leisurely stroll.

Taking Toddlers Outside

Toddlers take great delight in movement of all kinds—running, climbing, tumbling on the ground. You won't have many leisurely moments with this group; you've got to go at their pace, and it sometimes seems they never walk when they can run.

You don't need a lot of equipment in a backyard. There's lots to keep toddlers amused, as long as you join in and keep an eye on things. Squat down on the ground and look at the fat worms or pretty leaves with him—just stop him before they go into his mouth. A pail or box is a fine place to put a collection of sticks, stones, seed pods, or leaves.

Any time you can spend outdoors with toddlers is a bonus. Even fifteen minutes on a cold day gives them a chance to do all that running and screaming they can't work off indoors. Simple games of chase and tag are favorites.

Most toddlers can kick and throw a ball, but they're not very good at catching, so try rolling it to them when it's your turn. They may spend quite a while racing around on a tricycle or other riding toy; make sure it doesn't get out of control and head toward the street.

If a toddler is allowed to play in the lawn sprinkler, go ahead and join him. Watch out for moving parts, which can cause a nasty bruise. If there is a kiddie pool, it can be your best ally on hot summer days. Young children never seem to tire of sloshing in water; in fact, it may be hard to get them out.

But do be aware of the danger. Many small children drown every year in six inches or less of water. It's easy for them to slip and inhale a mouthful of water, and then they get too confused and scared to push themselves up out of trouble.

Never turn your back on a toddler in a pool, even for a moment, and stay close at hand all the time. Even when he's not in the pool, if there's any water in it, the same danger exists. He can race over and fall while you're retying your shoelace. Being aware of this potential deathtrap can prevent a tragic accident.

A trip to the playground is a big event to a toddler. There's so much to do that he sometimes can hardly decide where to begin. He may go down the slide once, move on to a few quick swings, and then race off to the sandbox. Your job is to keep up with him—it's easy to lose track of one small body in a crowded playground—and to offer help on equipment he can't handle alone. Going down the slide with you a few times may give him the courage to do it on his own.

Playgrounds are not really as fraught with danger as you might think. Youngsters are fairly cautious about using equipment that's much too difficult for them, and the few inevitable falls rarely do much damage. Do be prepared, though, to snatch up a toddler as he charges in front of the swings; he doesn't know enough to look and the child on the swing won't be able to stop.

If there's a sandbox, remember to bring some of your charge's toys with you. It will help resolve the frequent disputes over who uses what shovel if you can offer the child his own toy or trade for a while with another toddler.

Kids sometimes want to rest awhile, sitting on a bench with you and sampling any snacks you've brought along. But try not to let them get overtired. Toddlers may not know when to quit, so you might have to make that decision for them. When little Ted starts to stumble as he climbs the slide steps, it's time to go home. And of course be extra careful to hold his hand if you cross any streets.

You may be pretty exhausted yourself after an afternoon with an exuberant toddler, but you'll both have had a great time!

Taking Older Children Outside

Children of seven or older often have their own things to do, places to go, people to see. They don't need you tagging along. But before they bound out of the house, be sure both of you are clear about where they can go and what time they have to be home. Let them know you'll be there in case one of them scrapes a knee or needs a peanut butter and banana sandwich.

Younger children (ages three to seven) too may not want you to actually play with them, especially if there's a group of neighborhood friends. But do keep an eye on them to make sure they don't wander off after a lost ball or get into more mischief than they can handle.

If they don't have plans of their own, there are lots of things you can do with older children outside. Build a snowman in the winter. Play some sidewalk games—hopscotch, jump rope, jacks, or one, two, three, O'Leary—or just play catch. Budding athletes are often grateful for a chance to improve their catching and batting skills, and you can keep pitching to them as long as your arm holds out.

If a group of neighborhood kids has congregated in the backyard and they don't seem to have much to do, go out and get them started on Simon says. Dredge up your own old favorites and teach them to play Mother, may I? or statues or red rover or spud. You don't actually have to play yourself, but you may be called on to referee or clarify the rules.

What if it's a beautiful Saturday and the kids have been glued to the TV set for two hours? Suggest that you all take your lunch outside and have a picnic—the fresh air will do everyone good.

The parents may have suggested that you take the kids on an expedition—to the zoo, the library, a museum, or even an amusement park. Make sure you have enough money to pay for bus fares and any entrance fees and so on. You probably won't be doing this with more than two kids or with very young children, but even older ones can get lost in unfamiliar places. That can be pretty scary for both of you. So stay together and you can all enjoy it.

If you do go out somewhere with the children, it's a good idea to leave a note for their parents. Tell them where you're going and what time you'll return. If you can't get back on time, call and let them know everything is okay.

In the summer you may be asked to spend a day with the children at the local municipal pool. This can really be a pleasure. Before you set out, though, make certain you know each child's swimming capabilities and what he is allowed to do. Can Timmy go off the high diving board? Must Suzie stay at the shallow end?

There will be a lifeguard at the pool, but that doesn't mean you can stretch out and work on your tan or chat with your friends. You're being paid to watch the children and play with them. Kids can get in trouble in the water awfully fast, and you can't be sure the lifeguard isn't worrying about someone else. Be prepared to jump in and pull a child out of danger. It's helpful to take the Red Cross lifesaving class, which is offered at many schools and Y's. Make sure you know where the kids are at all times.

If the house you're sitting at has a pool, find out what the rules are for using it. No matter what, you must be out there with the kids whenever they're in the pool. Make your own rule that when neighbor kids come over to swim, a responsible person must come along to watch them—you can't be responsible for the whole gang. If the parents say it's okay for the kids to go to a neighbor's pool, again you must go with them and be there at all times. If two-year-old Joey is still taking his nap, the others will just have to wait until he wakes up. This may all sound a little heavy, but there's no replacement for a drowned child. Pools are a lot of fun, but they also can be very dangerous.

Safety Checklist

Here are some safety tips for the outdoors that you should commit to memory:

- Make sure babies don't put potentially dangerous things into their mouths—stones, berries, leaves, sticks, and so on.

• Don't let children get too much sun in hot weather.

• Keep the safety straps of a stroller fastened at all times.

• Never turn your back on a baby in a stroller.

• Be especially careful when crossing streets.

• Never leave or turn away from children in or around a pool or other body of water.

• Make sure you watch carefully when children play in a playground.

Let's Eat!

Mealtime is a good time to relax and talk with children. If you're easygoing about it, you can all sit down and have a pleasant lunch or dinner. You'll have to follow parents' instructions on what to feed the children, but don't be upset if the kids don't eat much. Some children don't eat as well when their parents aren't around, or they just may not be very hungry. Don't try to make them eat; be encouraging but let them stop when they want to.

Give yourself enough time to get food ready. You might give the kids some warning so they can finish up their game while you're getting lunch set up. Younger children can come and play with something at the kitchen table or on the floor so you can keep an eye on them. With any age group, observe elementary safety precautions: keep pot handles turned away from the front of the stove and don't leave hot pans and sharp knives within reach.

Feeding Babies

If the baby still takes a bottle, find out all about it—how to sterilize or heat it if necessary, how to mix formula, and so on. If you heat it, be sure to test a couple of drops on the inside of your wrist or forearm. When you start to feed the baby, the milk should feel neither hot nor cold on your skin.

You also need to know if the baby can hold the bottle himself, and how he lets you know he's thirsty.

You'll have to hold a tiny baby yourself or put him in the infant seat if that's what the parents prefer. To feed the baby on your lap, first settle yourself comfortably in a chair with arms so you'll have support for your elbow. Make sure there's a washcloth and a clean diaper or towel handy, and put the baby's bib on. Hold the baby so his head is higher than the rest of him and he's resting securely against the crook of your arm. Tilt the bottle enough so that he's getting only liquid, not air.

When he pushes the nipple out of his mouth, he's had enough for a while. Support him in a sitting position on your lap or hold him against your shoulder and pat or rub his back gently until he burps. (By the way, some babies don't burp— after five minutes if nothing happens, go ahead and put the bottle back in his mouth.)

Some babies bring up a little food when they burp or after they eat. They are not sick or throwing up; it's just that their digestive systems aren't fully mature yet and they regurgitate some of the food that goes down. Don't let it bother you. Wipe it up and go on with the feeding.

For babies who get more than a bottle at mealtime, prepare the cereal or strained food in advance. Then you won't have to interrupt the feeding. Put only small amounts on the spoon and be ready to scrape most of it off his chin and back into his mouth. He'll no doubt manage to get food on his hands and in his hair as well, so keep the washcloth handy.

An older baby may sit in a highchair—be sure she's strapped in securely and wearing her bib. She may be starting to use a cup and a spoon herself, though most of the meal will still be finger food for her. Put very little liquid in the cup. You can always put in some more, and when it spills (it will) you'll have less to mop up.

If you don't get too unglued about the mess, you can have a lot of fun feeding a baby. It's the high point of her day, and she'll love you for being the one who provides it.

Changing the Baby

Many babies need a diaper change after their meals. Find out where the clean diapers are kept and what to do with the dirty ones and if you should use any baby powder or ointment. Before you take off the wet diaper, look at how it has been fitted on the baby. Then you'll know how to put on the dry one. Hold the baby's two feet with one hand and slip the diaper underneath her. Then fasten it at the sides. With cloth diapers, be very careful with the pins. Don't put them down where she can reach them. When you stick them through the diaper material, put your own hand between the diaper and the baby's skin. With disposable diapers, just make sure the tapes are securely stuck down.

If the baby's clothes are very dirty or wet, they should be changed as well.

Feeding Toddlers

These youngsters sit in highchairs to eat and do a lot of the feeding themselves, though they may want you to help. Ask Mom if the child is allowed to climb in and out of the highchair by herself.

Get her meal together before you strap her in; she knows highchair time is food time and will probably get quite fussy if she has to sit there all ready while you're still scrambling her egg. She may not be able to talk well yet, so stay alert for her only half-verbal signals. If she looks around in bewilderment or frustration as you place her meal on her tray, you may have forgotten *her* spoon. Sit down facing the highchair and offer your assistance if she's having any trouble. You'll probably want to keep her milk cup off the highchair tray except when she's actually drinking—her coordination is improving but it's not perfect yet. Don't make too much of spills when they happen; mop them up and go on with lunch.

Toddlers can only concentrate on one thing at a time, so

try not to play games during mealtime. Laughing or giggling with a mouth full of food can cause a child to choke. Peek-a-boo can become more interesting than eating, and games can quickly end up with food and cup thrown on the floor.

Some children this age eat a lot and others eat very little. Start with a small amount of food in the child's dish; you can always dole out more. When the child starts pushing the food around and mashing it with her fingers, accept her decision that the meal is over. Wipe her face and hands and put her down. Cajoling her to eat more won't get you anywhere and both of you will get irritated. If she refuses everything but she hasn't eaten since breakfast, a handful of dry Cheerios and raisins will put something in her tummy to tide her over until dinner. But don't give a toddler nuts or popcorn or other small hard things to eat—she can't chew them very well and she's likely to swallow them whole or choke on them.

Toddlers are mostly cheerful and enthusiastic. Sharing their mealtime is great fun, though you have to be prepared to share a bite of your own sandwich too.

Feeding Older Children

Older children can pretty much feed themselves, but you may have to prepare the food. You may think that what they choose to eat is disgusting—dill pickles and peanut butter?—but as long as their mother said it was okay, shut your eyes and give it to them. Just remember all those strange combinations of foods you used to adore!

Youngsters like to feel responsible; they also like to feel they know more than you. You don't have to invent jobs for them. Get them to help at mealtime. They'll be able to tell you where things are kept and they'll set the table and show you what to put where. Make the preparations a group project, and you'll all be able to sit down and enjoy a civilized meal and conversation.

Rita Leydon

Food for Thought

Usually when you have to feed the children you're sitting for, their mother or father has provided something to give them. But sometimes parents forget, or are delayed in getting home. And sometimes the kids refuse to eat what you planned to feed them. What do you do then?

Don't panic. There's always something in the refrigerator or cupboard. You'll be able to put together a meal the kids will like without filling them up on Hershey bars and cookies.

Cereal. This may not sound like much of a supper to you, but toddlers and preschoolers would often just as soon eat cereal any time of day. Slice a banana into it if there's one handy; check the cupboard for raisins and add a handful to the bowl. This is a very easy meal to prepare, and it's also reasonably nutritious.

Canned foods: soup, spaghetti, baked beans, etc. Look in the cupboard to see what's available; then check with the kids to see what they like. Open the can and follow the directions on the label—it could hardly be easier!

Sandwiches.

• Lunch meat or cheese: be sure to ask the kids if they want mustard, ketchup, or mayonnaise on their bread.

• Peanut butter and jelly: is there a child anywhere who doesn't like this combo? You might suggest a new treat like peanut butter with sliced banana or applesauce.

• Grilled cheese: all you need is a heavy frying pan, bread, butter, and cheese. Butter two slices of bread and put the sliced cheese on top of one. Cover this with the other piece of bread, butter side up. Turn the heat on under the frying pan and put the sandwich in upside down (so the butter is on the bottom). Pat some butter on the top side while the underside is cooking; then turn it over after a few minutes. (*Tips*: if you use a lid the cheese will melt faster. Put some mustard on one slice of bread for a zing. Try a slice of tomato inside the sandwich.) Grilled cheese sandwiches and hot soup make a tasty and filling cold-weather meal.

Scrambled eggs. Allow two eggs for older children, one for the younger ones. Crack the eggs in a bowl, add a little milk, whisk it all with a fork. Place a pat of butter in a skillet and turn on the heat. When the butter is melted, dump in the eggs. Mix them around with the fork or turn them over with a spatula when they look "set" around the edges. Stir or turn the eggs until they are cooked. This is a real quickie—it takes about ten minutes from start to finish. Stick some bread in the toaster before you put the eggs in the skillet so it will be done at the same time. If there's fruit in the house (fresh or canned), it's great for dessert.

French toast. If you can find bread, butter, an egg, some milk, and a skillet, you're in business. Just beat the egg and some milk together in a pie plate with a fork (as if you were making scrambled eggs). Melt a couple of pats of butter in the skillet and dip a slice of bread in the egg mixture so that both sides are coated. Put this bread in the skillet and fry it on both sides until it's golden brown. One egg with milk is enough "batter" for three to four slices of bread. Plan on one or two slices for each child and don't forget yourself! If you can't find syrup, try spreading jelly or jam or sprinkling cinnamon and sugar on the hot French toast.

Hot dogs. Are you getting desperate—the kids are hungry but they don't like anything you suggest? Look in the freezer. There may be a package of hot dogs. You don't have to defrost them; just slam the package on the counter to break the hot dogs apart. Take out as many as you need and put the rest in a plastic bag back in the freezer. Put two or three inches of water in a saucepan and add the hot dogs. Set the pan on the stove, turn the heat up high, and in about ten minutes they'll be done.

Can't find the buns? Wrap each hot dog diagonally in a slice of bread. (If you can find toothpicks, use them to pin the overlapping corners together on top of the hot dog.) Tell the kids these are called "pigs in blankets"!

A Word About Choking

Children do choke on food from time to time. Often this is just "swallowing something the wrong way." You've probably experienced this yourself and you know that coughing makes it better. Let the child cough until he feels he can breathe freely and then wait a few minutes before giving him any more food or liquid.

You can lessen the chance of this happening by encouraging kids to conform to ordinary table manners. Tell them to chew with their mouths closed, not to talk or laugh with their mouths full, and to take small bites and chew them thoroughly —you've heard these rules of politeness a thousand times, but did you realize that they are safety measures as well?

It is possible that a child will choke on something and be unable to cough it up. If he can't cough, speak, or breathe, you've got to move fast. After breathing stops, only about five minutes of life remain. Get him out of his highchair or seat as quickly as possible and help him.

There are two methods of dealing with a person who cannot breathe because he has swallowed something that is blocking his air passage. First, try slapping him sharply two or three times on the back. The idea is to dislodge whatever is obstructing his breathing. For an infant, lay him facedown on your forearm with your hand under his face. Tilt him slightly so his head is lower than his feet and hit him firmly between the shoulder blades four times with your open palm. With an older child, stand behind him and support him with one arm across his chest. Give him four *sharp* blows between the shoulder blades.

If this doesn't work, use the second technique. This involves applying sudden sharp pressure to the front of the body rather than the back. For an older child, you continue to stand behind him and put both arms around him. Place one fist against the soft area just below the point where the ribs end in the center of the chest. Put your other hand over your fist and push in quickly and hard four times. This pressure forces the air out of the chest and, along with it, the object that is blocking the breathing.

For an infant, turn him faceup onto your other forearm. Use two or three fingers of the other hand to press firmly four times against the same soft muscle area below the center of the ribs.

If the child still is not breathing, use one hooked finger to reach into his throat and try to remove the object. Keep repeating this sequence of actions until the object is no longer blocking the child's breathing. He may spit out the object or swallow it. In either case, as soon as he is breathing regularly, call the doctor.

This all sounds pretty drastic, but you won't ever have to do it except in a dire emergency. If a child is not breathing, you've got to do something fast. You won't have time to call the doctor or anyone else first. So it's important to know what to do yourself for that one time in a million that it happens.

Suds and Sweet Dreams

Bedtime can sometimes be a troublesome time for children and therefore for you. It's perfectly understandable that kids who are having fun don't want to miss out on whatever may be going on. Even infants know that bedtime means the end of the bright lights and entertainment.

Some children too may feel a little nervous about being alone in a dark room with only a stranger in the house. Others may fear that Mom and Dad won't return; it's hard for them to believe in a future event they don't see with their own eyes.

And, of course, some kids may just want to see if you'll let them get away with more than their parents do.

There are ways of handling the whole bedtime procedure that can make it easier and more pleasant for everybody.

Putting Babies to Bed

One young mother came home at midnight to find her five-month-old son crying and the babysitter close to tears herself.

"I've tried everything to get him to go to sleep and nothing seems to work! He's fine until I put him down and then he starts to cry."

71

The mother took one look at her howling son lying on his back in the crib. "Oh dear, I forgot to tell you. He always sleeps on his stomach and he can't turn over yet!"

This story has two morals. The sitter should have found out about the baby's sleeping habits before the mother left. In addition, when he didn't drop off to sleep, she should have tried doing things differently instead of using the same approach over and over.

A baby's world is fairly limited, and each detail of it is very important to him. If you're sure he's not in pain from a diaper pin or an unburped air bubble in his tummy, try changing some of the elements of his sleep environment. Did you put his teddy bear in bed next to him? If you tucked his blanket in tightly, untuck it—he may need to kick his legs freely. Did you leave him uncovered? Some babies like to feel cozy. Maybe you just forgot to wind up his musical mobile before you turned out his light and left the room.

Babies are usually ready for sleep at bedtime. If you think about what might be bothering him, you can usually solve the problem and he'll doze off happily.

Before putting him to bed, you'll change his diaper and put on his nightclothes. You probably won't be giving an infant a bath; if you are asked to, be sure you know exactly how it's done. Bathing a baby is a tricky and slippery business. A sponge bath with a wet washcloth will do just as well to get the food off his face, hands, and neck and to clean up a messy bottom.

Get his bedroom ready—pull the curtains, turn on the nightlight or vaporizer, take the daytime toys out of the crib and put his bed companions in.

Now it's time to turn out the light and spend a few quiet moments together. Rocking him in the rocking chair, singing a lullaby, or rhythmically stroking him as he lies in his crib are all good ways to settle him down and provide a pleasant transition from activity time to sleeptime.

Naptime for babies is pretty much the same as bedtime, although it doesn't usually involve as much preparation. You'll change his diaper before putting him down, but many children don't wear pajamas for naps. Babies do go through phases of not wanting to nap, so be sure you know what to do if he doesn't fall asleep right away. Some mothers may tell you to let him cry himself to sleep, while others may prefer that you pick him up after five or ten minutes of screaming.

Once you've sat for a baby a few times, you'll get to know his routine. At the beginning, follow the parents' instructions as closely as you can. If you love to play with little babies, it's disappointing to have to put them to bed five minutes after you arrive. But don't let yourself be tempted to keep the baby up. He may be very happy to play with you, but his parents won't thank you when he's cranky the next day.

After he goes to sleep, if his door is closed (and be sure to ask about this) you can open it so you'll hear him if he cries. Go in and check on him now and then unless the parents specifically told you not to, but don't go in so often that he can't get a wink of sleep!

Putting Toddlers to Bed

This is the age of complicated and lengthy bedtime rituals. It doesn't mean much to a toddler when you say, "Fifteen more minutes, then bed," but going through her ritual with her gives her the signal that it's time for sleep.

Some toddlers have more elaborate bedtime procedures than others, but nearly all have something to do that's very important to them—saying good-night to their stuffed animals, turning out the light themselves before climbing into bed, reading a special story. Find out from the parents what the child's pattern is, since she's probably unable to explain it to you herself.

Most toddlers love baths, so be sure to leave enough time for them to play in the tub. You must stay in the bathroom with them at all times, so see whether it's all right for the children to take their baths together. Use your own good judgment about bathtub safety: don't let them fool with the hot water faucet or stand up in the tub. Keep play from getting too wild.

You will have found out from the parents how far along the child is in her toilet training and what you are supposed to do. Then it's time for pajamas. A balky child won't even notice that the pj's are going on if you do "this little piggy went to market" while you're buttoning.

Bedtime rituals can be fun, and cuddling up together with a favorite storybook makes you both feel good. But do stick to the parents' usual limits. The child would like you to read every story on the bookshelf, but when you say, "No, two stories is all for tonight," she's likely to accept it without a fuss—she knows the rules too.

When it's time, give her an extra hug and kiss and then leave the room. Your attitude of cheerful firmness will let her know this is really bedtime, even if she's whimpering a bit. If she gets up, don't try to bargain or compromise—reasoning with this age group doesn't accomplish anything. Don't even think about trying "just one more story." Take her back to bed and give her a little cuddling if she's feeling forlorn; then say good-night. Even if this happens several times, follow the same routine—she'll eventually give up.

Putting Older Children to Bed

Even children who can tell time may mysteriously forget how as bedtime approaches. Give them some warning: "Bedtime in twenty minutes, kids" will at least give them a chance to finish up their games or projects. Or you can plan things in advance so their baths are taken care of before their favorite TV program starts; then you can let them know that when it's over, it's bedtime. Keep an eye on things so that another game or TV program doesn't get under way at this point, providing an excuse to stay up longer.

Depending on their age, older kids may not want you to stay with them while they bathe, but do stay nearby so you can hear them the whole time.

Procrastination is the name of the game with many children at bedtime. You can hold this down to a minimum by moving them along through their bedtime preparations in a positive, cheerful manner. Promise a story or one chapter of a longer book or a little chat *after* they're in bed. Stay with them for ten or fifteen minutes while they get settled and then say good-night and leave. You can't make a child go to sleep but you can get him into bed. Then, if he says he's not sleepy, tell him that's fine, he can just lie in bed with the lights off and think about his plans for the next day or whatever. Don't let yourself get angry or annoyed. You probably did the same sort of thing yourself when you were younger. Just be firm and friendly. Bedtime is the time to get into bed and turn out the lights.

Bad Dreams and Nightmares

Children do occasionally have nightmares. If you hear a child cry or call out in fear after he's been asleep for a while, go in and find out what's wrong. Sit on the bed and hold him; if he wants to tell you about the dream, listen sympathetically. If you try to reassure him too soon ("There are no dinosaurs in Boston"), you won't get through to him. The dream dinosaur was real to him and he has to get it out of his system. When he begins to wind down, comfort him. Assure him that it was only a dream and that you'll be within call if he needs you. You might sit with him for a few minutes if he's still fearful.

Good-bye and Good Luck!

Babysitting is a job that carries a lot of responsibility. But your responsibility only extends so far. It's not your job to take the place of the parents and to change or criticize their ways of raising their children. Even if you don't agree (you may think it's not good for eight-year-old Jimmy to stay up watching TV till midnight), go along with the way the parents want things done. After all, they're not your children, and they may become very confused or upset if the rules are suddenly changed.

If you are in doubt about how to handle something, it's best to go easy rather than to be too strict or harsh. Actual punishment should be left up to the parents to decide on.

On the other hand, you are entitled as babysitter to have a few rules of your own. There's no reason for you to be taken advantage of—don't be afraid to say no. A young child pummeling you with his fists probably doesn't mean to hurt you, but it does hurt and you can tell him that hitting is not allowed. Don't get angry; just tell him pleasantly how things are going to be done while you're in charge.

Suppose a problem comes up that you're not sure how to handle, but it isn't something serious enough to call the children's parents about. Why not call your own parents? Take advantage of that fund of experience they accumulated raising you and your brothers and sisters. They'll probably be flattered that you asked their advice and they'll be happy to help you out.

When you babysit, treat the house you're in as if you were a guest. Clean up after yourself and use coasters for cups or glasses so you won't leave rings on the tabletops. Don't use fancy equipment like stereos or tape decks unless the parents have told you it's okay. If you must smoke, don't do it until after the children are in bed; be sure all the ashes are out, and clean up the dirty ashtray before the parents return. You should never drink anything stronger than soft drinks or coffee.

Above all, try to recall how you felt when you were younger, and treat your charges the way you would have liked to be treated. Kids are human beings too, even though sometimes you may wonder about that. Babysitting is full of unexpected pleasures and rewarding moments. The best part is when you arrive to see those smiling faces and hear the kids shouting happily, "Hey, Mom, the babysitter's here!"

PART III
You, the Professional

First - Aid Information

Most of the inevitable everyday accidents that befall children are not very serious. There may be a lot of tears and even some blood, but half an hour later the whole thing is forgotten.

However, serious accidents do sometimes happen and they require immediate action and professional help. It's a good idea to know what to do in various emergency situations.

If a Child Stops Breathing

In this situation, you don't have time to call anyone. You must try to get air into and out of the child's lungs as soon as possible. If he has choked on something, see page 67. If he's not breathing for any other reason—drowning, electric shock, massive allergic reaction, etc.—start mouth-to-mouth resuscitation. This involves blowing air gently and rhythmically into the child's mouth and nose.

This technique can be learned in first-aid or lifesaving classes or from a manual. Everyone should learn and practice it in case of an emergency anywhere.

Once the child is breathing, call an ambulance.

Note: If the child has received an electric shock, you must break the contact before you do anything else. Don't touch the child yourself until you are certain the electricity is off. Pull out the plug or push the child away from the source of electricity with a wooden broom handle, wooden chair, or other nonconductive item.

When to Call an Ambulance

If any child you're babysitting for suffers one of the following:

- Severe loss of blood

- Loss of consciousness

immediately call the emergency number for an ambulance. This is usually the fire department, paramedic service, or the police department. If you can't find these numbers, call the operator and tell her it's an emergency.

What do you say?

- That you are the injured child's sitter

- The nature of the problem

- The child's age

- The address and phone number of the house

- Your name and the family's name

Don't hang up—let the emergency person end the call. If he or she can tell you what to do for the child while you're waiting, listen carefully and follow instructions.

After you've called for help, here are some first-aid measures you can take.

For serious loss of blood: Try to stop the bleeding by applying pressure directly on the wound. Use a sterile gauze pad or clean piece of cloth—dish towel, diaper, sanitary napkin, bath towel—folded into a thick pad to press over the wound. If nothing else is available, use the palm of your hand. Elevate the injured part if possible and apply firm pressure continuously until help arrives. If the first pad fills with blood, add another on top of it—removing it may increase the flow of blood. (Don't attempt to use a tourniquet—this is an extremely dangerous procedure when done by an amateur.)

For loss of consciousness: You must make sure the child can breathe; you should also apply pressure to stop any bleeding and cover the child lightly to keep him warm. Do not move him at all except to ease his breathing or to stop bleeding. It is generally recommended that you turn the child gently on his back and tilt his chin up to keep his air passages open.

As soon as you've called, stay with him until help arrives. If he vomits, turn his head to one side and clear his mouth so he won't choke on the vomit.

When to Call the Doctor

In the situations listed on the preceding pages, a few minutes can mean the difference between life and death. There are other serious accidents that are not immediately life-threatening—you have a little more time to decide what to do.

Call the doctor right away if:

> • **The child is burned or scalded.** For the most serious (third-degree) burns, in which the skin is actually charred, don't try any first aid before calling the doctor. If you can't reach him immediately, call the fire department or emergency ambulance service.
> For a second-degree burn (one that blisters) that covers more than a very small spot, place the burned area under or in cold water and then call the doctor. Never

put any kind of grease or ointment or first-aid cream on these burns.

(For first-degree burns, see page 89.)

• **The child has swallowed a poisonous substance** (bleach, detergent, nail polish remover, medicines, rubbing alcohol, cosmetics, furniture polish, etc.). Lots of household products are poisonous to children; if you're in any doubt at all about whether a substance is poisonous or whether the child has actually swallowed some, call the doctor. Don't try to make the child vomit. Give him as much water or milk to drink as you can. Take the container and the child with you to the phone. If you can't speak to the doctor quickly, call the Poison Control Center listed in the front of the phone book.

Most poisons don't work instantaneously, so you have a little time. Give the doctor as much information as you can about what the child has swallowed and how much, then follow his or her instructions.

• **The child has a serious cut.** Blood is spurting from the wound and/or you can see the bone. Here again, try to stop the bleeding by pressing a pad of clean cloth on the wound. Take the child with you to the phone so you can keep applying pressure while you call.

• **The child has swallowed a sharp or pointed object.** Don't give him bread or do anything else. Take him with you to the phone so you can watch for any problems.

• **The child has injured his eye or ear.** This is one situation where you don't immediately apply pressure if it's bleeding. It's very hard to tell whether these injuries are serious or not, so keep the child from touching or rubbing it. Take him with you to the phone so you can describe the injury as well as possible.

• **You suspect the child has a broken bone.** Tell the child to stay where he is and not to move at all while you're calling the doctor. Describe the injury as well as you can and follow the doctor's instructions. Don't try to splint it without instructions.

When you call a child's pediatrician, you will probably reach an answering service at night or a secretary during office hours. Here's what to say:

• This is an emergency

• You are the child's babysitter

• The child is a patient of Dr. X (give the child's first and last names and his age)

• Briefly describe what has happened

• Give the phone number of the house you're in

• Ask if you can speak to the doctor now or if he will call you back right away

Try to be as clear as you can about all this and don't waste time on unimportant details.

After you've talked to the doctor and followed any instructions he may give you, call the child's parents. Explain what has happened and what you have done so far, and pass on what the doctor has told you. Be as calm as you can so they won't panic needlessly.

Your first concern is always the child, and your attitude can help him a lot. He's probably both frightened and in pain. Be as calm and reassuring as you can while you do whatever the doctor has advised. If there's nothing to do but wait, sit beside him and keep talking to him. Your comforting presence will make him feel he has help in facing his pain and fear.

Things to Handle Yourself

Practically every accident that happens while you're babysitting will be quite minor and you'll be able to give first aid yourself. In fact, it may only be a matter of "a kiss to make it better."

If it's something that needs attention, such as a Band-Aid or cold compress, be sure you tell the parents about it when they come home. A hard bump against a corner of a table may turn into an ugly black-and-blue spot by morning, and the parents will be alarmed if they don't know how it happened. If you're at all worried, call the parents at the number they left for you; explain what happened and tell them how the child seems now. Then they can decide whether to come home early or not. Don't hesitate to do this; even if they decide it's nothing to be concerned about, they'd rather have you be overcautious about their child's safety and well-being. If the parents can't be reached and you're still worried, call the child's doctor.

Some Common Childhood Mishaps

• **Bumps and bruises.** For the most part you won't do anything about this. If it's very painful or starting to swell up, wrap some ice in a washcloth or dish towel and hold it against the bruise to numb it slightly and reduce the swelling.

• **Abrasions** (skinned knees and elbows, etc.). These are painful but not serious. Wash the area carefully with soap and warm water (be sure to wash your own hands first); if there is dirt, sand, cinders, or the like stuck to the open wound, let the child soak it in the tub or a sinkful of water. It's important to get it clean, but you don't have to scrub it. When it's clean, pat the edges dry. Cover it with a Band-Aid if it will be rubbed by the child's clothes; otherwise, leave it open (it will heal faster). Don't put anything (iodine, mercurochrome, antibiotic ointment, etc.) on the abrasion, only soap and water.

• **Cuts.** Wash with soap and water and cover with a Band-Aid. If the cut is bleeding more than just a little, press a clean cloth to it until the bleeding stops, then wash and bandage.

Some cuts can't be bandaged. For cuts on the lip or inside the mouth, use ice or cold wet cloths. Scalp cuts bleed a lot, even when they're not very big. You won't be able to bandage them, since the adhesive won't stick to the child's hair. Wash the cut and press a clean cloth over it—try ice or a cold compress to stop the bleeding. If the cut is big enough to need bandaging, call the child's parents; they may want to have a doctor look at it and tape it up.

Deep cuts on a child's face should also make you call the parents since these can leave scars. And any cuts around a child's eyes can be potentially serious, so call the parents about these too.

• **Puncture wounds.** Kids jab themselves with all kinds of things—pins, compass points, any pointed object. Wash thoroughly with soap and water and leave the wound uncovered.

If the object was large (like a nail) or found outdoors, call the parents after you've washed the wound. They will want to make sure the child has had a recent enough tetanus shot. For smaller punctures from indoor objects, you can wait to tell them until they get home.

• **Nosebleeds.** These can happen when a child has a cold or has been sneezing a lot, or he may simply be prone to getting nosebleeds. There are two basic techniques doctors recommend for stopping nosebleeds. For both methods, have the child sit upright with his head bent forward. Either pinch the nostrils closed and hold them that way for five or ten minutes, or leave the nose alone and apply an ice pack (ice cubes wrapped in a cloth) to the child's upper lip or the bridge of his nose.

Once the bleeding stops, don't let the child blow his nose or touch it at all. It can very easily start bleeding again, so play a quiet game to keep him from too much activity for a half hour or so.

If the bleeding isn't pretty well stopped after fifteen minutes, call the child's parents.

• **Splinters.** If the end of the splinter is sticking out of the skin, you'll probably be able to pull it out with tweezers. Don't let the child touch the splinter while you look for the tweezers—he may break off the end and make things more difficult. Clean the tweezers with rubbing alcohol or soap and hot water. Then grasp the end of the splinter and pull it out gently in the same direction it went in.

If the splinter is all the way under the top layer of skin (so you can't grasp the end), the only way to get it out is with a clean needle. Don't try this unless you've done it on yourself and you have steady hands.

Sometimes soaking the child's hand or foot in hot water will loosen the skin enough so you can push the splinter partway out and then use the tweezers.

If you don't get the splinter out, be sure to tell the parents when they get home.

• **Swallowing smooth foreign objects** (buttons, fruit pits, marbles, coins). Many children have swallowed such objects with no ill effects. As long as the object is not sharp and the child has actually swallowed it (and not choked on it), there's no immediate danger. Take away any other similar items and call the parents to tell them about it. Don't give the child any kind of laxative or other medication.

• **Falls.** Toddlers and older children fall all the time without any problems. As long as the child picks himself up and is back to his normal playing within a few minutes, there's nothing to worry about.

Occasionally a child who falls while running full tilt has the wind knocked out of him. It's scary, because he can't get his breath for a moment, but it's not at all dangerous. Just comfort him and send him back to his game.

Babies also do fall, even if you're very careful. If the baby falls off the bed, don't panic. As long as he starts crying within a few seconds and has no obvious cuts or broken bones (this is highly unlikely), there's no cause for alarm. Pick him up and comfort him, then call his parents. Even though these falls almost never cause any injuries at all, many parents want to reassure themselves by talking to a doctor right away.

• **First-degree burns.** Most children learn the word *hot* very early. But occasional minor burns do happen, even if you're watching children carefully. Such burns only redden the skin and do not form blisters. Run cold water on a minor burn for five minutes or so, or hold the burned part in a bowl of ice water. This will stop the pain. If it's still bothering the child a lot, dab a little Vaseline on it. Be sure to tell the parents what happened when they get home.

• **Bee stings.** Though painful, bee and wasp stings are not dangerous unless a child is allergic or is stung many times.

For a single sting, pull out the stinger with tweezers if it's in the skin. Then use ice or ice water to stop the pain. If the stung area starts to itch, slather on a paste made of cornstarch or baking soda and a little water, or try calamine lotion. Be sure to tell the child's parents about it—stings may swell up a lot overnight.

For multiple bee stings, even if the child seems all right, call the doctor for advice.

• **Bites (animal and human).**
Pets and domestic animals: Today there is very little

danger of rabies from the bite of a pet dog or other animal. Laboratory-bred pets such as gerbils or hamsters do not carry rabies. But with dogs and cats that run around outdoors, there is always a slight possibility that it has been bitten by a wild animal with rabies. Therefore, if a child is bitten by a neighborhood dog, make certain you know who owns it and where it lives.

Treat an animal bite like other puncture wounds. Wash it thoroughly with soap and water and do not cover it with a bandage unless it is bleeding a lot. Animals may carry disease germs other than rabies, and leaving the wound open helps prevent infection.

When you've cleaned the bite, call the child's parents right away and tell them what has happened.

Wild animals: There is always a danger of rabies from the bite of any small wild animal. Therefore, don't let children feed squirrels or play in thick underbrush.

If at all possible, capture or kill the animal so it can be tested for rabies; if the animal is not rabid, the child will not have to go through the painful series of preventive shots. However, don't get bitten yourself in the process.

In any case, if the bite has broken the skin even slightly, wash it thoroughly and notify the parents and the doctor at once.

Snakebite: If you live in an area where poisonous snakes are often seen, you should have a snakebite kit and know how to use it. Do this for your own protection as well as the children's.

Human bites: This may sound a little strange, but young children do sometimes bite one another when playing in a sandbox or at home. Treat these bites like any animal bite. Human beings have many kinds of bacteria in their mouths that can cause infection. Wash the bite well, leave it uncovered, and call the parents.

Books on First Aid and Child Care

The more you know about caring for children, the better you'll be at it and the more relaxed you'll feel. There are lots of good books that can give you more information to help you do your job well. Most are available in libraries; some you may decide to buy for yourself in paperback.

First Aid and Medical

American National Red Cross. *Standard First Aid and Personal Safety.* Garden City, N.Y.: Doubleday & Co., Inc., 1975.
> This is the standard work on first aid. It's easy to read and not too long; it's a good book to study, even if you don't plan to babysit.

Pomeranz, Virginia E., M.D., and Dodi Schultz. *The Mothers' Medical Encyclopedia.* New York: New American Library (paperback), 1972.
> An alphabetical listing of practically everything that can happen to kids, this book gives commonsense advice on what to do about accidents and illness.

Child Care

Spock, Dr. Benjamin. *Baby and Child Care.* New York: Pocket
Books (paperback), 1976.
> This is it! It's still the standard reference book on
> children, and with good reason. It gives advice on
> medical and first-aid questions, as well as information
> on child development and answers to many minor but
> nerve-racking questions.

Child Development

Ilg, Frances L., M.D., and Louise Bates Ames, Ph.D. *Child Behavior.* New York: Harper & Row (paperback), 1972.
> Written by the directors of the Gesell Institute of
> Child Development, this book for parents contains
> more information than you probably need. But it's all
> interesting, and you can look up specific areas that
> you may have questions about, such as "Eating Behav-
> ior" or "Fears." You'll find suggestions for dealing
> with problems you may encounter.

More specific books on different age groups by Louise Bates
Ames and Frances L. Ilg are:
Your Two Year Old.
Your Three Year Old.
Your Four Year Old.
New York: Delacorte Press, 1976.
Pomeranz, Virginia E., M.D., with Dodi Schultz. *The First Five
Years: A Relaxed Approach to Child Care.* New York: Dell
Publishing Co. (paperback), 1976.
> Relaxed is the word here: this book is down-to-earth,
> practical, and even better, it's funny. Read it to reas-
> sure yourself that whatever problems you're running
> into are normal, and to pick up some sensible tips on
> solving them.

Information for
Your Own Safety

Unfortunately, some parents occasionally bypass your business relationship and act as though you are their girlfriend or boyfriend. They may make suggestive remarks or sexy jokes, or they may try to approach you in a way that's supposed to be "just friendly," but isn't.

This puts you in an awkward position. Usually there's nothing you can specifically complain about and you may wonder if you might be overreacting. But if it's making you nervous, say so. "Mr. Jones, please don't do that; it makes me very uncomfortable." You don't have to say anything more, and it's better not to get involved in a discussion.

This should solve the problem. If he was just being friendly, he may think you're oversensitive, but that's all right. If it continues, don't babysit for that family anymore. Be sure you are not doing anything to inadvertently encourage this type of behavior.

Another infrequent occurrence is the parents arriving home inebriated. A person under the influence of alcohol is in no state to drive you home safely, but he or she may not recognize that fact. This too puts you in a difficult position. You don't want to ride home with a drunk driver; on the other hand, you don't want to embarrass the parent by saying so or start an argument when he insists he's perfectly capable of driving safely.

It's best not to discuss this at all. Have a prearranged signal with your parents, so when you call home and say, "I'm ready to be picked up now," your own parents will know that you need a ride and won't ask questions about it on the phone. If they can't pick you up themselves, they can ask a neighbor to drive them over.

This will probably never happen to you. But if it ever does, don't let a fear of hurting someone's feelings make you take chances with your own life.

Client Bonus:
Sitter's Memo Pad

Here's a terrific, easy-to-make gift for your regular clients. It's something they can really use and it will keep them calling you for babysitting jobs. Make one for each of your best clients and then you can give them out as holiday gifts. You can make them as plain or fancy as you like. Here's how to do it.

What You Need

- A piece of sturdy cardboard at least 8" × 10" (be sure to take into consideration how much wall or table space your client has by the phone)

- Contact paper—enough to cover the cardboard on one side (get some that will go well with your client's decor)

- A pad of lined paper 4" × 6" or a bit smaller (be sure the paper tears off at the top)

- A thick rubber band about as long as the notepad is wide

- 2 bobby pins or large paper clips

- A piece of string or yarn 15" to 20" long

- A sharpened pencil

- A 3″ × 5″ file card

- Transparent tape

- Ice pick or other sharp implement to punch holes

How to Make It

Cover the cardboard neatly with the contact paper. Bring the paper around the edges a bit to keep them from shredding.

Center the small pad in the lower half of the cardboard (be sure to leave room below it for your own name and phone number). Punch a hole through the cardboard next to each top corner of the pad. Push one end of the rubber band through each hole from the front; at the back, slide each loop of the rubber band halfway up a bobby pin so it won't slip through the hole.

Copy the form on each page of the memo pad. You can use carbon paper and a ballpoint pen if you like, or you can write each page out individually. When it's done, attach the memo pad to the cardboard by slipping the cardboard back of the memo pad under the rubber band.

Now write the emergency information neatly on the file card; you can make it decorative if you like, but be sure the information is legible. Then tape the file card to the top part of your cardboard. Write your own name and phone number on a slip of paper and tape it to the bottom of the cardboard.

Punch a hole in the upper right-hand corner of the cardboard. Tie the string or yarn to the pencil and thread the free end through the hole, knotting it at the back to hold it in place.

If the sitter's memo pad is to hang on a wall, you can attach a glue-on picture hook to the back of it. Or run another piece of string or yarn across the top so it can hang on a nail or tack. Your clients will be delighted with this easy way to keep organized, and they'll think of you every time they need to call a babysitter.

EMERGENCY INFORMATION

Client's Name_____ Client's Phone Number _____

Client's Address _____

_____

Fire Dept. Phone Number _____

Ambulance Phone Number _____

Police Dept. Phone Number _____

Poison Control Center Phone Number _____

Client's Family Doctor's Name and Phone Number _____

_____

Client's Neighbor's Name and Phone Number _____

_____

MESSAGE PAD

WHERE WE ARE _____

_____

TIME WE'LL BE HOME _____

SPECIAL INSTRUCTIONS _____

_____

MESSAGES _____

_____

Your Name _____ Your Phone Number _____

Index

PART IV

Client Worksheets

Client Worksheets

Name _____

Address (and how to get there) _____

_____

_____

Phone Number _____

Children's Names and Ages _____

_____

_____

Rates Charged _____

EMERGENCY INFORMATION

Your Phone Number _____

Client's Doctor's Name and Phone Number _____

Your Doctor's Name and Phone Number _____

Client's Emergency Phone Number _____

Fire Department _____ Police Department _____

Ambulance _____ Poison Control Center _____

APPOINTMENT SCHEDULE

DATE	TIME OF ARRIVAL	EXPECTED TIME OF DEPARTURE	TRANSPORTATION HOME	AMOUNT EARNED

Special Instructions or problems (e.g., medication, allergies, special diet) ___

_____

_____

_____

_____

NAPTIME CHECKLIST   (For Babies and Toddlers)

When does child nap and for how long? _____

Does he sleep on his back or stomach? _____

Does baby wake and then go back to sleep on his own? _____

What does he wear for napping? _____

Must he stay in bed even if he doesn't sleep? _____

Any special rituals before or after napping? _____

Are shades or curtains drawn for naps? _____

Is door kept open or shut? _____

MEALTIME CHECKLIST

What should the children eat? _____

_____

When and where do they eat? _____

_____

How does everything work (highchair, stove, bottle warmer)? _____

_____

_____

_____

Do they have special dishes, glasses, silverware, bibs? _____

_____

Can they eat by themselves or must I feed them? _____

May they have more food if they want it? _____

Must they finish the meal before having dessert? _____

What happens if a child isn't hungry or doesn't want to eat? _____

_____

What about snacks, sweets, and soft drinks? _____

_____

_____

May they eat while watching television? _____

Are children expected to help at mealtimes (set the table, clean up afterward,
  fix their own sandwiches)? _____

_____

What may I fix to eat for myself? _____

_____

BATHTIME CHECKLIST

Do the children need baths? _____

Do they take baths together? _____

What kind of bathtub play is permitted (how much splashing)? _____

_____

How long may they stay in the tub? _____

Do I need to be in the bathroom with older children? _____

May they use bubble bath? _____

Which are their towels? _____

If bathroom door locks, how does it work? Do the children know how to

    lock it? _____

_____

BEDTIME CHECKLIST

What is each child's bedtime? _____

How strictly are bedtimes observed? _____

What are bedtime rituals (story, song, prayers, favorite toy, tooth brushing,

    toilet)? _____

_____

_____

May the children have snacks before bed? _____

_____

Where are nightclothes kept? _____

Should windows be open or closed? _____

Do they sleep with a light on? _____

Do they often wake up at night? If so, what should be done? _____

_____

_____

Is door kept open or shut? _____

INDOOR PLAY CHECKLIST

Where do the children do most of their playing (basement recreation room,

    own bedrooms, living room)? _____

_____

Is there anyplace they're not allowed to play? _____

_____

Is there any furniture they're to be especially careful of? _____

_____

Is there a special procedure for protecting floors or tables when coloring, pasting, and cutting? _____

What about other potentially messy play? _____

_____

Are they allowed snacks while they play and if so, must these snacks be eaten in the kitchen? _____

Are they allowed to watch TV? Is there a special program they like to watch? Any forbidden programs? _____

_____

Are they allowed to use the phonograph? Do they have their own or may they use their parents'? Do they know how to work it themselves? What records may they use? _____

_____

What are the rules about active play inside (running, ball throwing, roughhousing)? _____

(If there are two or more children) Is there anything that the big ones are allowed to do that the little ones are not, or vice versa? _____

_____

Are they expected to put their own toys away before they go to bed? Are building block constructions or models allowed to stay up? _____

_____

Are children allowed to use the phone? _____

OUTDOOR PLAY CHECKLIST

Where are the children allowed to play (yard, playground)? _____

_____

What outdoor clothes should they wear, and where are they kept? _____

_____

Where are outdoor toys kept? _____

May older children go outdoors by themselves? Which streets are they
   allowed to cross? What time must they be home? _____
_____

Are there rules about the use of bicycles, tricycles, etc.? _____
_____

Are older children allowed to go to a friend's house? If so, when should they
   come home? _____

Do younger children know how to use playground equipment? Do they need
   help on the slide, etc.? Is there some equipment they're not allowed to
   use? _____
_____

May children play in messy areas (sandbox, puddles, mud)? _____
_____

Are children allowed to play in the lawn sprinkler or wading pool? _____
_____

If there is a backyard or neighborhood swimming pool, are they allowed to
   use it? _____

Can they swim? Do they need life jackets? _____

Do they need protection from the sun (sunscreen lotion, shirt, hat)? _____
_____

Can they play outside in the snow? What equipment can they use? _____
_____

If the stroller is collapsible, how does it work? _____
_____
_____

Client Worksheets

Name _____

Address (and how to get there) _____

_____

_____

Phone Number _____

Children's Names and Ages _____

_____

_____

Rates Charged _____

EMERGENCY INFORMATION

Your Phone Number _____

Client's Doctor's Name and Phone Number _____

Your Doctor's Name and Phone Number _____

Client's Emergency Phone Number _____

Fire Department _____ Police Department _____

Ambulance _____ Poison Control Center _____

APPOINTMENT SCHEDULE

DATE	TIME OF ARRIVAL	EXPECTED TIME OF DEPARTURE	TRANSPORTATION HOME	AMOUNT EARNED

Special Instructions or problems (e.g., medication, allergies, special diet) _____

_____

_____

_____

_____

NAPTIME CHECKLIST   (For Babies and Toddlers)

When does child nap and for how long? _____

Does he sleep on his back or stomach? _____

Does baby wake and then go back to sleep on his own? _____

What does he wear for napping? _____

Must he stay in bed even if he doesn't sleep? _____

Any special rituals before or after napping? _____

Are shades or curtains drawn for naps? _____

Is door kept open or shut? _____

MEALTIME CHECKLIST

What should the children eat? _____

_____

When and where do they eat? _____

_____

How does everything work (highchair, stove, bottle warmer)? _____

_____

_____

_____

Do they have special dishes, glasses, silverware, bibs? _____

_____

Can they eat by themselves or must I feed them? _____

May they have more food if they want it? _____

Must they finish the meal before having dessert? _____

What happens if a child isn't hungry or doesn't want to eat? _____

_____

What about snacks, sweets, and soft drinks? _____

_____

_____

May they eat while watching television? _____

Are children expected to help at mealtimes (set the table, clean up afterward, fix their own sandwiches)? _____

_____

What may I fix to eat for myself? _____

_____

BATHTIME CHECKLIST

Do the children need baths? _____

Do they take baths together? _____

What kind of bathtub play is permitted (how much splashing)? _____

_____

How long may they stay in the tub? _____

Do I need to be in the bathroom with older children? _____

May they use bubble bath? _____

Which are their towels? _____

If bathroom door locks, how does it work? Do the children know how to

    lock it? _____

_____

BEDTIME CHECKLIST

What is each child's bedtime? _____

How strictly are bedtimes observed? _____

What are bedtime rituals (story, song, prayers, favorite toy, tooth brushing,

    toilet)? _____

_____

_____

May the children have snacks before bed? _____

_____

Where are nightclothes kept? _____

Should windows be open or closed? _____

Do they sleep with a light on? _____

Do they often wake up at night? If so, what should be done? _____

_____

_____

Is door kept open or shut? _____

INDOOR PLAY CHECKLIST

Where do the children do most of their playing (basement recreation room,

    own bedrooms, living room)? _____

_____

Is there anyplace they're not allowed to play? _____

_____

Is there any furniture they're to be especially careful of? _____

_____

Is there a special procedure for protecting floors or tables when coloring,
pasting, and cutting? _____

What about other potentially messy play? _____

_____

Are they allowed snacks while they play and if so, must these snacks be eaten
in the kitchen? _____

Are they allowed to watch TV? Is there a special program they like to watch?
Any forbidden programs? _____

_____

Are they allowed to use the phonograph? Do they have their own or may they
use their parents'? Do they know how to work it themselves? What
records may they use? _____

_____

What are the rules about active play inside (running, ball throwing,
roughhousing)? _____

(If there are two or more children) Is there anything that the big ones are
allowed to do that the little ones are not, or vice versa? _____

_____

Are they expected to put their own toys away before they go to bed? Are
building block constructions or models allowed to stay up? _____

_____

Are children allowed to use the phone? _____

OUTDOOR PLAY CHECKLIST

Where are the children allowed to play (yard, playground)? _____

_____

What outdoor clothes should they wear, and where are they kept? _____

_____

Where are outdoor toys kept? _____

May older children go outdoors by themselves? Which streets are they
    allowed to cross? What time must they be home? _____

_____

Are there rules about the use of bicycles, tricycles, etc.? _____

_____

Are older children allowed to go to a friend's house? If so, when should they
    come home? _____

Do younger children know how to use playground equipment? Do they need
    help on the slide, etc.? Is there some equipment they're not allowed to
    use? _____

_____

May children play in messy areas (sandbox, puddles, mud)? _____

_____

Are children allowed to play in the lawn sprinkler or wading pool? _____

_____

If there is a backyard or neighborhood swimming pool, are they allowed to
    use it? _____

Can they swim? Do they need life jackets? _____

Do they need protection from the sun (sunscreen lotion, shirt, hat)? _____

_____

Can they play outside in the snow? What equipment can they use? _____

_____

If the stroller is collapsible, how does it work? _____

_____

_____

Client Worksheets

Name _____

Address (and how to get there) _____

_____

_____

Phone Number _____

Children's Names and Ages _____

_____

_____

Rates Charged _____

EMERGENCY INFORMATION

Your Phone Number _____

Client's Doctor's Name and Phone Number _____

Your Doctor's Name and Phone Number _____

Client's Emergency Phone Number _____

Fire Department _____ Police Department _____

Ambulance _____ Poison Control Center _____

APPOINTMENT SCHEDULE

DATE	TIME OF ARRIVAL	EXPECTED TIME OF DEPARTURE	TRANSPORTATION HOME	AMOUNT EARNED

Special Instructions or problems (e.g., medication, allergies, special diet) ____

_____

_____

_____

_____

NAPTIME CHECKLIST (For Babies and Toddlers)

When does child nap and for how long? _____

Does he sleep on his back or stomach? _____

Does baby wake and then go back to sleep on his own? _____

What does he wear for napping? _____

Must he stay in bed even if he doesn't sleep? _____

Any special rituals before or after napping? _____

Are shades or curtains drawn for naps? _____

Is door kept open or shut? _____

MEALTIME CHECKLIST

What should the children eat? _____

_____

When and where do they eat? _____

_____

How does everything work (highchair, stove, bottle warmer)? _____

_____

_____

_____

Do they have special dishes, glasses, silverware, bibs? _____

_____

Can they eat by themselves or must I feed them? _____

May they have more food if they want it? _____

Must they finish the meal before having dessert? _____

What happens if a child isn't hungry or doesn't want to eat? _____

_____

What about snacks, sweets, and soft drinks? _____

_____

_____

May they eat while watching television? _____

Are children expected to help at mealtimes (set the table, clean up afterward, fix their own sandwiches)? _____

_____

What may I fix to eat for myself? _____

_____

BATHTIME CHECKLIST

Do the children need baths? _____

Do they take baths together? _____

What kind of bathtub play is permitted (how much splashing)? _____

_____

How long may they stay in the tub? _____

Do I need to be in the bathroom with older children? _____

May they use bubble bath? _____

Which are their towels? _____

If bathroom door locks, how does it work? Do the children know how to

lock it? _____

_____

BEDTIME CHECKLIST

What is each child's bedtime? _____

How strictly are bedtimes observed? _____

What are bedtime rituals (story, song, prayers, favorite toy, tooth brushing,

toilet)? _____

_____

_____

May the children have snacks before bed? _____

_____

Where are nightclothes kept? _____

Should windows be open or closed? _____

Do they sleep with a light on? _____

Do they often wake up at night? If so, what should be done? _____

_____

_____

Is door kept open or shut? _____

INDOOR PLAY CHECKLIST

Where do the children do most of their playing (basement recreation room,

own bedrooms, living room)? _____

_____

Is there anyplace they're not allowed to play? _____

_____

Is there any furniture they're to be especially careful of? _____

_____

Is there a special procedure for protecting floors or tables when coloring, pasting, and cutting? _____

What about other potentially messy play? _____

_____

Are they allowed snacks while they play and if so, must these snacks be eaten in the kitchen? _____

Are they allowed to watch TV? Is there a special program they like to watch? Any forbidden programs? _____

_____

Are they allowed to use the phonograph? Do they have their own or may they use their parents'? Do they know how to work it themselves? What records may they use? _____

_____

What are the rules about active play inside (running, ball throwing, roughhousing)? _____

(If there are two or more children) Is there anything that the big ones are allowed to do that the little ones are not, or vice versa? _____

_____

Are they expected to put their own toys away before they go to bed? Are building block constructions or models allowed to stay up? _____

_____

Are children allowed to use the phone? _____

OUTDOOR PLAY CHECKLIST

Where are the children allowed to play (yard, playground)? _____

_____

What outdoor clothes should they wear, and where are they kept? _____

_____

Where are outdoor toys kept? _____

May older children go outdoors by themselves? Which streets are they
  allowed to cross? What time must they be home? _____

_____

Are there rules about the use of bicycles, tricycles, etc.? _____

_____

Are older children allowed to go to a friend's house? If so, when should they
  come home? _____

Do younger children know how to use playground equipment? Do they need
  help on the slide, etc.? Is there some equipment they're not allowed to
  use? _____

_____

May children play in messy areas (sandbox, puddles, mud)? _____

_____

Are children allowed to play in the lawn sprinkler or wading pool? _____

_____

If there is a backyard or neighborhood swimming pool, are they allowed to
  use it? _____

Can they swim? Do they need life jackets? _____

Do they need protection from the sun (sunscreen lotion, shirt, hat)? _____

_____

Can they play outside in the snow? What equipment can they use? _____

_____

If the stroller is collapsible, how does it work? _____

_____

_____

Client Worksheets

Name _____

Address (and how to get there) _____

_____

_____

Phone Number _____

Children's Names and Ages _____

_____

_____

Rates Charged _____

EMERGENCY INFORMATION

Your Phone Number _____

Client's Doctor's Name and Phone Number _____

Your Doctor's Name and Phone Number _____

Client's Emergency Phone Number _____

Fire Department _____   Police Department _____

Ambulance _____   Poison Control Center _____

APPOINTMENT SCHEDULE

DATE	TIME OF ARRIVAL	EXPECTED TIME OF DEPARTURE	TRANSPORTATION HOME	AMOUNT EARNED

Special Instructions or problems (e.g., medication, allergies, special diet) ____

_____

_____

_____

_____

NAPTIME CHECKLIST   (For Babies and Toddlers)

When does child nap and for how long? _____

Does he sleep on his back or stomach? _____

Does baby wake and then go back to sleep on his own? _____

What does he wear for napping? _____

Must he stay in bed even if he doesn't sleep? _____

Any special rituals before or after napping? _____

Are shades or curtains drawn for naps? _____

Is door kept open or shut? _____

MEALTIME CHECKLIST

What should the children eat? _____

_____

When and where do they eat? _____

_____

How does everything work (highchair, stove, bottle warmer)? _____

_____

_____

_____

Do they have special dishes, glasses, silverware, bibs? _____

_____

Can they eat by themselves or must I feed them? _____

May they have more food if they want it? _____

Must they finish the meal before having dessert? _____

What happens if a child isn't hungry or doesn't want to eat? _____

_____

What about snacks, sweets, and soft drinks? _____

_____

_____

May they eat while watching television? _____

Are children expected to help at mealtimes (set the table, clean up afterward,
    fix their own sandwiches)? _____

_____

What may I fix to eat for myself? _____

_____

BATHTIME CHECKLIST

Do the children need baths? _____

Do they take baths together? _____

What kind of bathtub play is permitted (how much splashing)? _____

_____

How long may they stay in the tub? _____

Do I need to be in the bathroom with older children? _____

May they use bubble bath? _____

Which are their towels? _____

If bathroom door locks, how does it work? Do the children know how to
    lock it?_____

_____

BEDTIME CHECKLIST

What is each child's bedtime? _____

How strictly are bedtimes observed? _____

What are bedtime rituals (story, song, prayers, favorite toy, tooth brushing,
    toilet)? _____

_____

_____

May the children have snacks before bed? _____

_____

Where are nightclothes kept? _____

Should windows be open or closed? _____

Do they sleep with a light on? _____

Do they often wake up at night? If so, what should be done? _____

_____

_____

Is door kept open or shut? _____

INDOOR PLAY CHECKLIST

Where do the children do most of their playing (basement recreation room,
    own bedrooms, living room)? _____

_____

Is there anyplace they're not allowed to play? _____

_____

Is there any furniture they're to be especially careful of? _____

_____

Is there a special procedure for protecting floors or tables when coloring,
    pasting, and cutting? _____

What about other potentially messy play? _____

_____

Are they allowed snacks while they play and if so, must these snacks be eaten
    in the kitchen? _____

Are they allowed to watch TV? Is there a special program they like to watch?
    Any forbidden programs? _____

_____

Are they allowed to use the phonograph? Do they have their own or may they
    use their parents'? Do they know how to work it themselves? What
    records may they use? _____

_____

What are the rules about active play inside (running, ball throwing,
    roughhousing)? _____

(If there are two or more children) Is there anything that the big ones are
    allowed to do that the little ones are not, or vice versa? _____

_____

Are they expected to put their own toys away before they go to bed? Are
    building block constructions or models allowed to stay up? _____

_____

Are children allowed to use the phone? _____

OUTDOOR PLAY CHECKLIST

Where are the children allowed to play (yard, playground)? _____

_____

What outdoor clothes should they wear, and where are they kept? _____

_____

Where are outdoor toys kept? _____

May older children go outdoors by themselves? Which streets are they
    allowed to cross? What time must they be home? _____

_____

Are there rules about the use of bicycles, tricycles, etc.? _____

_____

Are older children allowed to go to a friend's house? If so, when should they
    come home? _____

Do younger children know how to use playground equipment? Do they need
    help on the slide, etc.? Is there some equipment they're not allowed to
    use? _____

_____

May children play in messy areas (sandbox, puddles, mud)? _____

_____

Are children allowed to play in the lawn sprinkler or wading pool? _____

_____

If there is a backyard or neighborhood swimming pool, are they allowed to
    use it? _____

Can they swim? Do they need life jackets? _____

Do they need protection from the sun (sunscreen lotion, shirt, hat)? _____

_____

Can they play outside in the snow? What equipment can they use? _____

_____

If the stroller is collapsible, how does it work? _____

_____

_____

Client Worksheets

Name _____

Address (and how to get there) _____

_____

_____

Phone Number _____

Children's Names and Ages _____

_____

_____

Rates Charged _____

EMERGENCY INFORMATION

Your Phone Number _____

Client's Doctor's Name and Phone Number _____

Your Doctor's Name and Phone Number _____

Client's Emergency Phone Number _____

Fire Department _____ Police Department _____

Ambulance _____ Poison Control Center _____

APPOINTMENT SCHEDULE

DATE	TIME OF ARRIVAL	EXPECTED TIME OF DEPARTURE	TRANSPORTATION HOME	AMOUNT EARNED

Special Instructions or problems (e.g., medication, allergies, special diet) ____

_____

_____

_____

_____

NAPTIME CHECKLIST   (For Babies and Toddlers)

When does child nap and for how long? _____

Does he sleep on his back or stomach? _____

Does baby wake and then go back to sleep on his own? _____

What does he wear for napping? _____

Must he stay in bed even if he doesn't sleep? _____

Any special rituals before or after napping? _____

Are shades or curtains drawn for naps? _____

Is door kept open or shut? _____

MEALTIME CHECKLIST

What should the children eat? _____

_____

When and where do they eat? _____

_____

How does everything work (highchair, stove, bottle warmer)? _____

_____

_____

_____

Do they have special dishes, glasses, silverware, bibs? _____

_____

Can they eat by themselves or must I feed them? _____

May they have more food if they want it? _____

Must they finish the meal before having dessert? _____

What happens if a child isn't hungry or doesn't want to eat? _____

_____

What about snacks, sweets, and soft drinks? _____

_____

_____

May they eat while watching television? _____

Are children expected to help at mealtimes (set the table, clean up afterward,
    fix their own sandwiches)? _____

_____

What may I fix to eat for myself? _____

_____

BATHTIME CHECKLIST

Do the children need baths? _____

Do they take baths together? _____

What kind of bathtub play is permitted (how much splashing)? _____

_____

How long may they stay in the tub? _____

Do I need to be in the bathroom with older children? _____

May they use bubble bath? _____

Which are their towels? _____

If bathroom door locks, how does it work? Do the children know how to
    lock it? _____ _____

_____

BEDTIME CHECKLIST

What is each child's bedtime? _____

How strictly are bedtimes observed? _____

What are bedtime rituals (story, song, prayers, favorite toy, tooth brushing,
    toilet)? _____

_____

_____

May the children have snacks before bed? _____

_____

Where are nightclothes kept? _____

Should windows be open or closed? _____

Do they sleep with a light on? _____

Do they often wake up at night? If so, what should be done? _____

_____

_____

Is door kept open or shut? _____

INDOOR PLAY CHECKLIST

Where do the children do most of their playing (basement recreation room,
    own bedrooms, living room)? _____

_____

Is there anyplace they're not allowed to play? _____

_____

Is there any furniture they're to be especially careful of? _____

_____

Is there a special procedure for protecting floors or tables when coloring, pasting, and cutting? _____

What about other potentially messy play? _____

_____

Are they allowed snacks while they play and if so, must these snacks be eaten in the kitchen? _____

Are they allowed to watch TV? Is there a special program they like to watch? Any forbidden programs? _____

_____

Are they allowed to use the phonograph? Do they have their own or may they use their parents'? Do they know how to work it themselves? What records may they use? _____

_____

What are the rules about active play inside (running, ball throwing, roughhousing)? _____

(If there are two or more children) Is there anything that the big ones are allowed to do that the little ones are not, or vice versa? _____

_____

Are they expected to put their own toys away before they go to bed? Are building block constructions or models allowed to stay up? _____

_____

Are children allowed to use the phone? _____

OUTDOOR PLAY CHECKLIST

Where are the children allowed to play (yard, playground)? _____

_____

What outdoor clothes should they wear, and where are they kept? _____

_____

Where are outdoor toys kept? _____

May older children go outdoors by themselves? Which streets are they
  allowed to cross? What time must they be home? _____

_____

Are there rules about the use of bicycles, tricycles, etc.? _____

_____

Are older children allowed to go to a friend's house? If so, when should they
  come home? _____

Do younger children know how to use playground equipment? Do they need
  help on the slide, etc.? Is there some equipment they're not allowed to
  use? _____

_____

May children play in messy areas (sandbox, puddles, mud)? _____

_____

Are children allowed to play in the lawn sprinkler or wading pool? _____

_____

If there is a backyard or neighborhood swimming pool, are they allowed to
  use it? _____

Can they swim? Do they need life jackets? _____

Do they need protection from the sun (sunscreen lotion, shirt, hat)? _____

_____

Can they play outside in the snow? What equipment can they use? _____

_____

If the stroller is collapsible, how does it work? _____

_____

_____

Client Worksheets

Name _____

Address (and how to get there) _____

_____

_____

Phone Number _____

Children's Names and Ages _____

_____

_____

Rates Charged _____

EMERGENCY INFORMATION

Your Phone Number _____

Client's Doctor's Name and Phone Number _____

Your Doctor's Name and Phone Number _____

Client's Emergency Phone Number _____

Fire Department _____ Police Department _____

Ambulance _____ Poison Control Center _____

APPOINTMENT SCHEDULE

DATE	TIME OF ARRIVAL	EXPECTED TIME OF DEPARTURE	TRANSPORTATION HOME	AMOUNT EARNED

Special Instructions or problems (e.g., medication, allergies, special diet) ____

_____

_____

_____

_____

NAPTIME CHECKLIST (For Babies and Toddlers)

When does child nap and for how long? _____

Does he sleep on his back or stomach? _____

Does baby wake and then go back to sleep on his own? _____

What does he wear for napping? _____

Must he stay in bed even if he doesn't sleep? _____

Any special rituals before or after napping? _____

Are shades or curtains drawn for naps? _____

Is door kept open or shut? _____

MEALTIME CHECKLIST

What should the children eat? _____

_____

When and where do they eat? _____

_____

How does everything work (highchair, stove, bottle warmer)? _____

_____

_____

_____

Do they have special dishes, glasses, silverware, bibs? _____

_____

Can they eat by themselves or must I feed them? _____

May they have more food if they want it? _____

Must they finish the meal before having dessert? _____

What happens if a child isn't hungry or doesn't want to eat? _____

_____

What about snacks, sweets, and soft drinks? _____

_____

_____

May they eat while watching television? _____

Are children expected to help at mealtimes (set the table, clean up afterward, fix their own sandwiches)? _____

_____

What may I fix to eat for myself? _____

_____

BATHTIME CHECKLIST

Do the children need baths? _____

Do they take baths together? _____

What kind of bathtub play is permitted (how much splashing)? _____

_____

How long may they stay in the tub? _____

Do I need to be in the bathroom with older children? _____

May they use bubble bath? _____

Which are their towels? _____

If bathroom door locks, how does it work? Do the children know how to
  lock it? _____

_____

BEDTIME CHECKLIST

What is each child's bedtime? _____

How strictly are bedtimes observed? _____

What are bedtime rituals (story, song, prayers, favorite toy, tooth brushing,
  toilet)? _____

_____

_____

May the children have snacks before bed? _____

_____

Where are nightclothes kept? _____

Should windows be open or closed? _____

Do they sleep with a light on? _____

Do they often wake up at night? If so, what should be done? _____

_____

_____

Is door kept open or shut? _____

INDOOR PLAY CHECKLIST

Where do the children do most of their playing (basement recreation room,
  own bedrooms, living room)? _____

_____

Is there anyplace they're not allowed to play? _____

_____

Is there any furniture they're to be especially careful of? _____

_____

Is there a special procedure for protecting floors or tables when coloring, pasting, and cutting? _____

What about other potentially messy play? _____

_____

Are they allowed snacks while they play and if so, must these snacks be eaten in the kitchen? _____

Are they allowed to watch TV? Is there a special program they like to watch? Any forbidden programs? _____

_____

Are they allowed to use the phonograph? Do they have their own or may they use their parents'? Do they know how to work it themselves? What records may they use? _____

_____

What are the rules about active play inside (running, ball throwing, roughhousing)? _____

(If there are two or more children) Is there anything that the big ones are allowed to do that the little ones are not, or vice versa? _____

_____

Are they expected to put their own toys away before they go to bed? Are building block constructions or models allowed to stay up? _____

_____

Are children allowed to use the phone? _____

OUTDOOR PLAY CHECKLIST

Where are the children allowed to play (yard, playground)? _____

_____

What outdoor clothes should they wear, and where are they kept? _____

_____

Where are outdoor toys kept? _____

May older children go outdoors by themselves? Which streets are they
    allowed to cross? What time must they be home? _____
_____

Are there rules about the use of bicycles, tricycles, etc.? _____
_____

Are older children allowed to go to a friend's house? If so, when should they
    come home? _____

Do younger children know how to use playground equipment? Do they need
    help on the slide, etc.? Is there some equipment they're not allowed to
    use? _____
_____

May children play in messy areas (sandbox, puddles, mud)? _____
_____

Are children allowed to play in the lawn sprinkler or wading pool? _____
_____

If there is a backyard or neighborhood swimming pool, are they allowed to
    use it? _____

Can they swim? Do they need life jackets? _____

Do they need protection from the sun (sunscreen lotion, shirt, hat)? _____
_____

Can they play outside in the snow? What equipment can they use? _____
_____

If the stroller is collapsible, how does it work? _____
_____

_____

Client Worksheets

Name _____

Address (and how to get there) _____

_____

_____

Phone Number _____

Children's Names and Ages _____

_____

_____

Rates Charged _____

EMERGENCY INFORMATION

Your Phone Number _____

Client's Doctor's Name and Phone Number _____

Your Doctor's Name and Phone Number _____

Client's Emergency Phone Number _____

Fire Department _____ Police Department _____

Ambulance _____ Poison Control Center _____

APPOINTMENT SCHEDULE

DATE	TIME OF ARRIVAL	EXPECTED TIME OF DEPARTURE	TRANSPORTATION HOME	AMOUNT EARNED

Special Instructions or problems (e.g., medication, allergies, special diet) ____

_____

_____

_____

_____

NAPTIME CHECKLIST   (For Babies and Toddlers)

When does child nap and for how long? _____

Does he sleep on his back or stomach? _____

Does baby wake and then go back to sleep on his own? _____

What does he wear for napping? _____

Must he stay in bed even if he doesn't sleep? _____

Any special rituals before or after napping? _____

Are shades or curtains drawn for naps? _____

Is door kept open or shut? _____

MEALTIME CHECKLIST

What should the children eat? _____

_____

When and where do they eat? _____

_____

How does everything work (highchair, stove, bottle warmer)? _____

_____

_____

_____

Do they have special dishes, glasses, silverware, bibs? _____

_____

Can they eat by themselves or must I feed them? _____

May they have more food if they want it? _____

Must they finish the meal before having dessert? _____

What happens if a child isn't hungry or doesn't want to eat? _____

_____

What about snacks, sweets, and soft drinks? _____

_____

_____

May they eat while watching television? _____

Are children expected to help at mealtimes (set the table, clean up afterward,
    fix their own sandwiches)? _____

_____

What may I fix to eat for myself? _____

_____

BATHTIME CHECKLIST

Do the children need baths? _____

Do they take baths together? _____

What kind of bathtub play is permitted (how much splashing)? _____

_____

How long may they stay in the tub? _____

Do I need to be in the bathroom with older children? _____

May they use bubble bath? _____

Which are their towels? _____

If bathroom door locks, how does it work? Do the children know how to

lock it? _____

_____

BEDTIME CHECKLIST

What is each child's bedtime? _____

How strictly are bedtimes observed? _____

What are bedtime rituals (story, song, prayers, favorite toy, tooth brushing,

toilet)? _____

_____

_____

May the children have snacks before bed? _____

_____

Where are nightclothes kept? _____

Should windows be open or closed? _____

Do they sleep with a light on? _____

Do they often wake up at night? If so, what should be done? _____

_____

_____

Is door kept open or shut? _____

INDOOR PLAY CHECKLIST

Where do the children do most of their playing (basement recreation room,

own bedrooms, living room)? _____

_____

Is there anyplace they're not allowed to play? _____

_____

Is there any furniture they're to be especially careful of? _____

_____

Is there a special procedure for protecting floors or tables when coloring,
    pasting, and cutting? _____

What about other potentially messy play? _____

_____

Are they allowed snacks while they play and if so, must these snacks be eaten
    in the kitchen? _____

Are they allowed to watch TV? Is there a special program they like to watch?
    Any forbidden programs? _____

_____

Are they allowed to use the phonograph? Do they have their own or may they
    use their parents'? Do they know how to work it themselves? What
    records may they use? _____

_____

What are the rules about active play inside (running, ball throwing,
    roughhousing)? _____

(If there are two or more children) Is there anything that the big ones are
    allowed to do that the little ones are not, or vice versa? _____

_____

Are they expected to put their own toys away before they go to bed? Are
    building block constructions or models allowed to stay up? _____

_____

Are children allowed to use the phone? _____

OUTDOOR PLAY CHECKLIST

Where are the children allowed to play (yard, playground)? _____

_____

What outdoor clothes should they wear, and where are they kept? _____

_____

Where are outdoor toys kept? _____

May older children go outdoors by themselves? Which streets are they
    allowed to cross? What time must they be home? _____

_____

Are there rules about the use of bicycles, tricycles, etc.? _____

_____

Are older children allowed to go to a friend's house? If so, when should they
    come home? _____

Do younger children know how to use playground equipment? Do they need
    help on the slide, etc.? Is there some equipment they're not allowed to
    use? _____

_____

May children play in messy areas (sandbox, puddles, mud)? _____

_____

Are children allowed to play in the lawn sprinkler or wading pool? _____

_____

If there is a backyard or neighborhood swimming pool, are they allowed to
    use it? _____

Can they swim? Do they need life jackets? _____

Do they need protection from the sun (sunscreen lotion, shirt, hat)? _____

_____

Can they play outside in the snow? What equipment can they use? _____

_____

If the stroller is collapsible, how does it work? _____

_____

_____